TEACHING LITERACY IN THIRD GRADE

TOOLS FOR TEACHING LITERACY

Donna Ogle and Camille Blachowicz, Series Editors

This highly practical series includes two kinds of books: (1) grade-specific titles for first-time teachers or those teaching a particular grade for the first time; (2) books on key literacy topics that cut across all grades, such as integrated instruction, English language learning, and comprehension. Written by outstanding educators who know what works based on extensive classroom experience, each research-based 7" × 10" volume features hands-on activities, reproducibles, and best practices for promoting student achievement. These books are suitable as texts for undergraduate- or graduate-level courses; preservice teachers will find them informative and accessible.

TEACHING LITERACY IN SIXTH GRADE
Karen Wood and Maryann Mraz

TEACHING LITERACY IN KINDERGARTEN
Lea M. McGee and Lesley Mandel Morrow

INTEGRATING INSTRUCTION: LITERACY AND SCIENCE
Judy McKee and Donna Ogle

TEACHING LITERACY IN SECOND GRADE
Jeanne R. Paratore and Rachel L. McCormack

TEACHING LITERACY IN FIRST GRADE
Diane Lapp, James Flood, Kelly Moore, and Maria Nichols

PARTNERING FOR FLUENCY
Mary Kay Moskal and Camille Blachowicz

TEACHING LITERACY THROUGH THE ARTS
Nan L. McDonald and Douglas Fisher

TEACHING LITERACY IN FIFTH GRADE
Susan I. McMahon and Jacqueline Wells

TEACHING LITERACY IN THIRD GRADE
Janice F. Almasi, Keli Garas-York, and Leigh-Ann Hildreth

TEACHING LITERACY
in Third Grade

Janice F. Almasi
Keli Garas-York
Leigh-Ann Hildreth

Series Editors' Note by Donna Ogle and Camille Blachowicz

THE GUILFORD PRESS
New York   London

© 2007 The Guilford Press
A Division of Guilford Publications, Inc.
72 Spring Street, New York, NY 10012
www.guilford.com

Printed in the United States of America

This book is printed on acid-free paper.

Last digit is print number: 9   8   7   6   5   4   3   2   1

Library of Congress Cataloging-in-Publication Data

Almasi, Janice F.
  Teaching literacy in the third grade / by Janice F. Almasi, Keli Garas-York,
Leigh-Ann Hildreth.
     p. cm. — (Tools for teaching literacy)
  Includes bibliographical references and index.
   ISBN-13: 978-1-59385-359-4   ISBN-10: 1-59385-359-9 (pbk.: alk. paper)
   ISBN-13: 978-1-59385-360-0   ISBN-10: 1-59385-360-2 (cloth: alk. paper)
   1. Language arts (Early childhood) 2. English language—Composition
and exercises—Study and teaching (Early childhood) 3. Early childhood
education. I. Garas-York, Keli. II. Hildreth, Leigh-Ann. III. Title.
   LB1139.5.L35A46 2006
   372.6—dc22
                                                     2006027884

ABOUT THE AUTHORS

Janice F. Almasi, PhD, is the Carol Lee Robertson Endowed Professor of Literacy Education at the University of Kentucky, where she teaches courses in research and theory in literacy. She earned her PhD and MEd in reading education from the University of Maryland and her BS in elementary education from Edinboro University of Pennsylvania. Before becoming a university educator, Dr. Almasi was an elementary classroom teacher and a reading specialist in Maryland.

Keli Garas-York, PhD, is currently an assistant professor at Buffalo State College, Buffalo, New York, where she teaches undergraduate and graduate literacy courses. She was a reading specialist in the West Seneca Central School District, where she worked with students in kindergarten through grade 6 for 2 years. She also taught third graders in the Buffalo Public School System for 7 years. Dr. Garas-York earned her BS in elementary education from the State University of New York College at Oswego, her master's degree in special education from St. Bonaventure University, and her PhD in reading education from the State University of New York at Buffalo.

Leigh-Ann Hildreth, MEd, is a third-grade teacher in the Sweet Home Central School District, Amherst, New York. She earned her BS in elementary education from the State University of New York at Geneseo and her master's degree in elementary education from the State University of New York at Buffalo. She is a trained Reading Recovery teacher. Mrs. Hildreth successfully taught first graders for 8 years in the Sweet Home Central School District before changing grade levels 2 years ago, when she found herself teaching third graders for the first time in her career.

SERIES EDITORS' NOTE

As teacher educators and staff developers, we have become aware of the need for a series of books for thoughtful practitioners who want a practical, research-based introduction to teaching literacy at specific grade levels. Preservice and beginning teachers want to know how to be as effective as possible; they also know there are great differences in what students need across grade levels. We have met teacher after teacher who, when starting to teach or teaching a new grade, asked for a guide targeted at their specific grade level. Until now we have not had a resource to share with them.

We also collaborate with staff developers and study group directors who want effective inservice materials that they can use with teachers at many different levels yet that still provide specific insights for individual grade levels. Thus the Tools for Teaching Literacy series was created.

This series is distinguished by two innovative characteristics designed to make it useful to individual teachers, staff developers, and study groups alike. Each Tools for Teaching Literacy volume:

> ➤ Is written by outstanding educators who are noted for their knowledge of research, theory, and best practices; who spend time in real classrooms working with teachers; and who are experienced staff developers who work alongside teachers applying these insights in classrooms. We think the series authors are unparalleled in these qualifications.

> ➤ Is organized according to a structure shared by all the grade-level books with chapters on:

>> ▪ the nature of the learner at the particular grade level

>> ▪ appropriate goals for literacy

- setting up the physical environment for literacy
- getting to know students with appropriate assessments and planning for differentiation
- a week in the grade-level classroom—what this looks like in practice with important instructional strategies and routines
- resources for learning

With this common organization across the grade-level books, a staff developer can use several different volumes in the series for teacher study groups, new teacher seminars, and other induction activities, choosing particular discussion and learning topics, such as classroom organization, that cross grade-level concerns. Teachers can also easily access information on topics of most importance to them and make comparisons across the grade levels.

This researcher–teacher team has created a wonderfully rich introduction to third-grade children—helping all readers become more sensitive to their cognitive, social, emotional and academic development and needs. The authors also provide a clear and thorough explanation of approaches teachers can use to enhance their students' literacy development. A highlight of the book is the rich description of how instruction and assessment can be interrelated. The focus is on informal, ongoing assessments involving students in engaging, fun activities. From these and more diagnostic tools (including attitude and self-concept measures, informal reading inventories, and running records), teachers are shown how to think deeply about their students and differentiate instruction appropriately. New third-grade teachers can trust this guide to give them the foundation they need to be successful in developing students' literacy and creating a rewarding classroom experience.

DONNA OGLE
CAMILLE BLACHOWICZ

PREFACE

This volume came about as a collaborative effort among the three of us (Janice, Keli, and Leigh-Ann). We have known each other for more than 10 years in a variety of literacy contexts. We first met through our mutual participation in our local reading council, the Niagara Frontier Reading Council (NFRC), an affiliate of the New York State Reading Association and the International Reading Association. Through NFRC we have been able to work with literacy colleagues in western New York to learn more about literacy pedagogy and research. Janice and Leigh-Ann served on NFRC's Board of Directors and in various leadership roles (vice president, president-elect, president, and past president) in the 1990s. Keli assumed those same leadership roles in the early 2000s and is currently the president of NFRC. So, our commitment to service and leadership in the field of literacy led to a respect for one another's talents and forged lasting professional and personal friendships.

We came to realize that we had common interests in research-based literacy activities and a common vision for literacy instruction. As a professor at the State University of New York at Buffalo, Janice often visited local classrooms, provided professional development for teachers, and led teacher study groups related to literacy. Janice often visited Keli's and Leigh-Ann's classrooms and found not only their instruction but also their classroom environments to be extraordinary. Although they worked in different school districts, both Keli and Leigh-Ann exhibited a strong desire to examine their own teaching in more detail and wanted to learn more about literacy. Because of their leadership and encouragement, many other teachers in their districts joined them as they participated in study group sessions with Janice.

Keli, a long-time third-grade teacher in a large city, handled with flair and vigor the enormous challenges of working in an impoverished school with underserved populations of children. Her classroom was filled with dynamic lessons, motivated children, and a relentless pursuit of achievement. After many years of teaching and pursuing graduate studies part time, Keli turned her attention to full-time study as a doctoral student while attending the State University of New York at Buffalo, where Janice was a professor. Through their work at the university, Keli and Janice became collaborators in many research and writing endeavors. It was essential to represent in this text Keli's experiences and expertise as a long-time third-grade teacher.

Leigh-Ann, a first-grade teacher for years, shifted to third grade 2 years ago. Then, as now, literacy suffuses every aspect of her classroom and every minute of her day. Her experience in shifting from teaching first graders to teaching third graders was also essential to the creation of this text.

We hope this volume will give you the tools needed by a new teacher of third graders or an experienced teacher who is new to third grade. Chapter 1 provides a developmental overview of the cognitive, social, emotional, and affective characteristics of many third-grade learners. It is infused with personal anecdotes from authentic classroom experiences with third-grade learners to help you visualize the ways in which third graders think and act. However, we want to acknowledge from the onset that our descriptions are guidelines. Every third grader is unique. Therefore, the characteristics we describe in Chapter 1 are general and certainly will not apply to every third-grade learner.

Chapter 2 continues to offer developmental perspectives about third graders; however, it also provides specifics related to literacy development—word identification, fluency, comprehension, vocabulary, motivation, and writing. Although theoretical and research perspectives guide this work, it is infused with practical examples and provides a blueprint for planning appropriate instructional goals in each area of literacy.

Chapter 3 begins to get at the nuts and bolts of actually creating your classroom environment. It includes information related to physically arranging your classroom and designing your literacy program to motivate students, accommodate their developmental needs, and accomplish the goals described in earlier chapters. This chapter is full of practical ideas to help you design a literate environment and a literacy program including teacher read-alouds, shared reading, guided reading, and independent reading.

Chapter 4 provides an in-depth overview of various ways to assess your third graders. The emphasis in this chapter is on authentic, classroom-based assessments rather than standardized, formal assessments. Practical and exciting ways to assess word identification, fluency, comprehension, vocabulary, attitude/motivation, and writing are discussed. We also offer specific ways of using assessments within your literacy program (i.e., during teacher read-alouds, shared reading, guided reading, and independent reading).

Chapter 5 gives you a glimpse into Leigh-Ann's third-grade classroom. In this chapter you will see how she uses the theoretical and research-based ideas presented in the previous chapters as she takes you on a personal journey through her classroom. Her descriptions and dialogue will give you insight into how to create a lively, dynamic, and literacy-rich environment.

With our earlier caution about the uniqueness of every third grader in your classroom in mind, Chapter 6 tells how to individualize your instruction to meet the needs of all of your learners. It explains how to use the data you gather through assessments to evaluate your students' needs and develop appropriate, individualized goals for each learner. You will also learn how to plan in various increments (i.e., daily, by thematic units, and yearly) to meet your learners' needs.

Throughout the text we mention many resources to help create a literate environment in your third-grade classroom. Chapter 7 gathers these resources together so you can easily access information on how to locate texts and instructional activities. Along the way, we offer practical tips to help you learn how to gather even more resources.

Through our collaborative efforts over the years, each of us has grown as a reader, writer, thinker, and teacher. Our challenge was to represent what we know from theory and research about teaching third graders and ground it in practice. Keli's and Leigh-Ann's real-life experiences and voices as third-grade teachers give authenticity and credibility to this book. We hope it provides you with a sense not only of what is possible but also of what is very doable in your third-grade classroom.

JANICE F. ALMASI
KELI GARAS-YORK
LEIGH-ANN HILDRETH

ACKNOWLEDGMENTS

Many individuals contributed to the creation of this text, and although it was a collaborative endeavor, we have chosen to extend our personal gratitude individually rather than collectively:

I would first like to express my gratitude to Keli Garas-York and Leigh-Ann Hildreth. Your classrooms, your students, and you yourselves are the inspiration underlying this book. You are incredible teachers, colleagues, and friends. You cannot imagine how much your boundless enthusiasm, your consummate intellect, and your continual support have meant to me.

Angie Madden's generous contribution of time and talent in editing drafts of many of the chapters in this book is also greatly appreciated.

I want to thank Donna Ogle and Camille Blachowicz for the opportunity to contribute to their Tools for Teaching Literacy series. I appreciate their vision, their critical feedback, their trust, and their patience.

I am also indebted to The Guilford Press's Chris Jennison for his extraordinary guidance, which I cherish and respect. Also, I want to thank Craig Thomas and Guilford's talented editorial and production staff for bringing our text to life.

As always, I am indebted to my family—my mother and father, Jessie and John Almasi; my sisters, Judy Downing and JoAnn Suchko; and my brother, John Almasi. Your daily doses of patience, encouragement, support, and love are my source of strength.

—JANICE F. ALMASI

I am indebted to the many teachers and students with whom I have worked in the past 9 years. I owe many thanks to the educators and children from Broadway

Village Elementary School #57, who gently and not so gently helped me to become a more responsive and effective teacher. In particular, I wish to thank Catherine Benjamin, Rosemarie Tronolone, Debra Hurley, Jean Heyden, Kathy Zatkos, and Dawn Metzger. Thank you for your constant support, guidance, and humor. Also, I want to thank my colleagues at Winchester Elementary School, especially Kim McCartan and Brian Graham, from whom I have learned a great deal about meeting the needs of students. Thank you all for allowing me to be a part of your classrooms. I also want to express my gratitude to my professors at the University at Buffalo, especially Janice Almasi. Thank you for all of your wisdom, dedication, and patience. Finally, I would like to thank my family—Richard York, Tena Garas, Michael Garas, Amy Garas, Marie Dougherty, and Edward Garas—for all of their love and support.

—KELI GARAS-YORK

My heartfelt thanks go out to many individuals who contributed to my efforts in writing this book. I am fortunate to work alongside talented and dedicated colleagues at Maplemere Elementary School, who make teaching and learning fun. In particular, I wish to thank Jacquie Stablewski, Amy Canetti, June Peczkowski, and Ann Laudisio. Thank you for countless hours of great conversation, guidance, and, most of all, your friendship. I would also like to thank the wonderful parents and students with whom I have had the honor of working over the years. To the parents, thank you for sharing your beautiful children with me. And to the children, you are truly amazing individuals who constantly remind me of what is important. I want to thank my mentor and long-time friend Ardith Cole for the knowledge and support that she has so generously shared. Ardie has always made me feel much greater than I am. She is truly a brilliant and creative individual whom I have always counted on for everything. Also, I thank Janice Almasi for inviting me to join her in the writing of this book. Thank you for believing in me. Finally, I thank my family—Christopher Hildreth, Ashleigh Hildreth, Kayleigh Hildreth, Judy Hensal, Bob Hensal, and Beth Hensal—for their unconditional love and support.

—LEIGH-ANN HILDRETH

CONTENTS

CHAPTER 1

WHAT IS THE THIRD-GRADE LEARNER LIKE?

The other day, at a grocery store I rarely frequent, a young man approached me and asked if I was Miss Garas, his third-grade teacher. My mind quickly tried to picture the young man as a boy in order to figure out who he was. I guessed a name and was wrong. As soon as he told me his name was Jean-Pierre (a pseudonym), I knew him immediately. I asked him what he was doing. Fortunately, he was still in school (now in high school) and working at the grocery store. I asked about his younger brother, Pierre, and he, too, was in school. He explained that he had been living with his mother again but had recently moved in with his sister. His grandmother had moved to Atlanta. At the end of our short conversation, he gave me a big hug and I wished him well.

The rest of the evening, I thought about Jean-Pierre. He was in my classroom the very first year I started teaching. At the time, his mother was jumping between drug rehabilitation and incarceration. His grandmother took care of the three children and constantly struggled with the boys' difficult behavior. We had remained in close contact through the year.

That evening I reflected on how I had decided what Jean-Pierre needed from me as his teacher. For instance, how did I know what kind of support to give him regarding his family situation? How did I determine how to meet his needs academically? Of course, every student is different academically, emotionally, socially, culturally, and so on. We, as teachers, try to get to know our students as quickly as possible and assess their academic abilities in order to find out how to provide the best possible support and instruction for them. However, there are some general

1

developmental characteristics of third graders that can be used to help teachers make decisions about how to best meet their needs. In this chapter, we will briefly address the following developmental characteristics of third graders:

- ➤ Cognitive characteristics
- ➤ Social characteristics
- ➤ Emotional characteristics
- ➤ Affective characteristics

On average, students who are in third grade are 8 years old. Students between the ages of 7 and 10 may be third graders because of their birthdays, when they started school, or retention. For the most part, as we explore the developmental characteristics of third graders, we are talking about students who are in middle childhood (between the ages of 6 and 10).

COGNITIVE CHARACTERISTICS OF THIRD GRADERS

Research in psychology and education has given us a general sense of where third graders should be cognitively. Basic overviews of the work of Piaget and Vygotsky, as well as a brief discussion of the information-processing view and metacognition, will be used to describe, in general, the cognitive abilities of the third graders you might meet in your classroom.

Piagetian Perspectives

Piaget believed that the cognitive system "actively selects and interprets environmental information in the construction of its own knowledge rather than passively copying the information just as it is presented to the senses" (Flavell, 1985, p. 5). From this statement we can deduce that Piaget considered children to be active, motivated learners who organize what they learn from their experiences (McDevitt & Ormrod, 2002). This is important to consider as we delve deeper into Piaget's notions of cognitive development and think about our own students and how we plan instruction for them.

Piaget believed children not only learn from their experiences but also adapt to their environment through assimilation and accommodation processes. Assimilation refers to how children deal with a "new event in a way that is consistent with an existing scheme" or something they already know or have experienced (McDevitt & Ormrod, 2002, p. 112). Accommodation refers to how children deal with a "new event by either modifying an existing scheme or forming a new one" (p. 112). These processes can be related to how students deal with new information as they read.

Piaget also believed that interaction with the physical environment and other people is critical for cognitive development. The process of equilibration, or being able to explain new things based on what one already knows, or in terms of "existing schemes," promotes progression toward more complex thought forms (McDevitt & Ormrod, 2002, p. 113).

Piaget outlined four stages of cognitive development: the sensorimotor stage (birth to 2 years), the preoperational stage (2 years to 6–7 years), the concrete operations stage (6–7 years to about 10–12 years), and the formal operations stage (11–12 years through adulthood). As third-grade teachers, we should be most concerned about the concrete operations stage. Although there is some criticism of Piaget's notions of stages (Gelman & Baillargeon, 1983), we can use his descriptions to facilitate student growth in literacy.

Along with the more general notions of conservation, reversibility, reliance on logic versus perception, and decentration, which can affect a child's academic growth, characteristics of the concrete operations stage can directly affect his or her literacy development. For example, in middle childhood, children are less egocentric and are able to differentiate their own perspectives from those of others. Children are also able to reason deductively, drawing inferences from pieces of information (McDevitt & Ormrod, 2002). Mastery of these abilities allows most third graders to understand different viewpoints and draw conclusions as they read, write, speak, and listen.

During my fourth year of teaching, I (KG-Y) was asked to teach a split class of second and third graders. I was amazed at the differences between the two groups of students at the beginning of the school year. Many of the second graders were still in the preoperational stage and were still very egocentric. This made it difficult for some second graders to work in discussion groups or cooperative learning groups because they had difficulty seeing the views of other classmates. It was gratifying to see how quickly these students grew in their abilities to work together and participate in peer discussions of text with other second and third graders as they transitioned from preoperational to concrete operational thought. The students were able to transition to the concrete operational stage because they had an abundance of opportunities to work with one another, which reinforces Piaget's notion of the importance of interacting with others and the critical role it plays in cognitive development.

When concrete operational thought is compared to formal operational thought, it is easy to see why students sometimes say to teachers, "I don't get it!" Their thought processes, although they are developing, will most likely not reach the formal operational stage, which can be associated with the cognitive processes of most adults, until they are long gone from your classroom. For instance, most children in third grade rely more on concrete reality and have difficulty with the abstract. Therefore, if we are explaining a reading strategy to a child in third grade, we need to begin with concrete examples before moving into more abstract ideas or ways of thinking (Almasi, 2003).

Vygotskian Perspectives

Vygotsky's theory of cognitive development is often called the sociocultural perspective because he stressed the importance of society and culture in cognitive development (McDevitt & Ormrod, 2002). He believed that children's cognitive development could be fostered by adults or more knowledgeable peers who help them perform challenging activities successfully (Vygotsky, 1978). In addition to social interaction, Vygotsky discussed the importance of the tools the culture provides to help in the development of knowledge, attitudes, ideas, and values (Woolfolk, 1998).

Vygotsky (1978) stressed the importance of determining two developmental levels of a child. The first is the child's actual level of development, and the second is the highest level at which a child can be successful with assistance from others. The distance between these two levels is what Vygotsky described as "the zone of proximal development" (p. 86), which can define functions that are maturing.

In literacy instruction, the zone of proximal development allows us to identify what a child has already achieved developmentally and plan instruction to facilitate his or her growth from that point. As teachers who engage in literacy instruction, we can provide varying amounts of scaffolding according to students' needs to move them along cognitively. When I work with my students, I point out that we all have different strengths. I explain my own difficulties with mathematics but also discuss my love for reading and my achievements in that particular area. I try to make clear to students that there is a variety of talents among them. Thus they can learn from one another during cooperative learning activities, learning centers, and peer discussions.

Peer discussion is an example of a classroom activity to which Vygotsky's (1978) theory of development pertains. My third graders engaged in peer discussions of text three to five times a week. Peer discussions are opportunities for students to talk about what they find interesting or questions they have about a text (Almasi, 2003). These discussions with classmates allow students to learn from one another, to make connections with their own lives and with other texts. Peer discussions also give students the opportunity to practice their use of strategies, with assistance or scaffolding from other members of the group. Thus, in Vygotskian terms, while participating in peer discussions, students are able to observe their peers using cognitive (e.g., interpretive and comprehension strategies) and social (e.g., taking turns and staying on topic) tools inherent to the peer discussion culture. These tools may not be familiar to these students. That is, they may not be able to use these cognitive and social tools on their own when they read and interpret text. But over time, as they continue to observe their peers, some students will begin to try out some of these tools. By observing and gradually participating in the social setting (i.e., peer discussion), these students will gradually learn, or internalize, how to use these new cognitive tools to help them interpret text.

My favorite example of such gradual internalization is a peer discussion involving three of my students, Angel, Quanita, and Ja'Rell. The children were reading a story in which a dog is missing on a boat. Quanita began talking about how she and her family brought her aunt's dog on a boat. She went into some detail. Ja'Rell interrupted her and told her she was getting off track. Angel quickly jumped in, explaining to both Ja'Rell and Quanita how Quanita was tapping into her background knowledge. Whereas Ja'Rell felt that Quanita had violated a social rule (i.e., sticking to the topic), Angel was able to see how Quanita's cognitive tool use (i.e., tapping into background knowledge) was relevant in helping the group come to a deeper understanding of the text. Allowing students to work together in such groups can give them the chance to discuss what they are learning.

Vygotsky stressed the importance of language for cognitive development. Woolfolk (1998) noted that "Vygotsky believed that language in the form of private speech (talking to yourself) guides cognitive development" (p. 45). "Self-talk eventually evolves into inner speech: Children 'talk' to themselves mentally rather than aloud. They continue to direct themselves verbally through tasks and activities, but others can no longer see and hear the means by which they do it" (p. 132). The language experiences available in a social setting, such as peer discussion provide students with opportunities to observe the cognitive processes others use as they try to make sense of text. According to Vygotsky, eventually such cognitive processes evolve into inner speech. That is, after observing and gradually participating in social settings such as peer discussion, students will eventually internalize the same cognitive thought processes to which they were exposed.

As adults, the processes we use to understand what we read or to figure out unknown words are for the most part automatic. It is helpful for teachers to make these mental processes known to students, so that they are able to integrate similar processes in their own thinking and problem solving. Students can be given access to their teacher's thought processes through think-alouds, a "metacognitive technique or strategy in which a teacher verbalizes thoughts aloud while reading a selection orally, thus modeling the process of comprehension" (Harris & Hodges, 1995, p. 256). Students are able to hear how a teacher walks herself through understanding what she is reading step by step. Students will gradually internalize these steps, initially using self-talk, and then begin to use them on their own. Think-alouds will be discussed in greater detail in Chapter 4.

Because language plays such a large role in cognitive development, according to Vygotsky (1978), it is crucial for teachers to provide students with ample opportunities for verbalization (Almasi, 2003). As teachers, we need to think about who is doing most of the talking in our classrooms. If most of the talk is teacher talk, we should consider allowing more opportunities for our students to talk with one another and reflect aloud on their own learning.

McDevitt and Ormrod (2002, pp. 132–134) summed up Vygotsky's key ideas of cognitive development:

> ➤ Complex mental processes begin as social activities; as children develop, they gradually internalize the processes they use in social contexts and begin to use them independently.

> ➤ Through both informal interactions and formal schooling, adults convey to children the ways in which their culture interprets and responds to the world.

> ➤ Children can perform more challenging tasks when assisted by more advanced and more competent individuals.

> ➤ Challenging tasks promote maximum cognitive growth.

What this means for our classrooms is that literacy instruction for third graders should include opportunities for social interaction and verbalization. Students should be given challenging activities with the appropriate support from adults or more knowledgeable individuals in order to internalize something new or to learn to independently use a new strategy.

Information-Processing View

The information-processing view is a group of theories dealing with the ways children gain, ponder, alter or add on to, and remember information as they develop (McDevitt & Ormrod, 2002). Those who view cognition from this perspective often use the computer as a model for the way the mind works (Woolfolk, 1998). Information is taken into the mind (a sensory register). Perception then helps determine what information might be used and stores it in the working memory. When the information is totally processed, it is stored in long-term memory, where it can be retrieved in the future.

One aspect of the information-processing theory relevant to learning deals with attention. It is believed that attention plays a major role in how information is interpreted and stored. Attention allows information to move from the sensory register to the working memory. To accommodate this move, teachers need to constantly monitor students' attention. If students are not attending, they are not likely to remember the lesson. Fortunately for most students, distractibility tends to decrease as they advance in elementary school and their attention becomes more purposeful (McDevitt & Ormrod, 2002).

Many observations from the information-processing perspective that can affect reading development and achievement have been made about students in middle childhood. Children's ability to attend to important stimuli and ignore unimportant stimuli gradually increases, so they are better able to concentrate on such tasks as reading for a specific purpose, identifying unknown words, or making sense of text. Gradually basic skills become automatic. In reading, this means that as such skills as identifying unknown words become more automatic, cognitive space and effort once dedicated to word identification are no longer needed, leaving more space for other cognitive processes—similar to the notion of freeing up space on your computer's hard drive. As children grow as readers and spend less mental effort on word identification, they can put more effort into understanding what they are reading. Moreover, their knowledge base expands as they are exposed to environments other than school and home (McDevitt & Ormrod, 2002). Students in middle childhood are able to see connections between different aspects of their lives and the world around them. This developmental change in middle childhood can affect the background knowledge students bring to texts. These notions are important to keep in mind as we plan the length of a lesson, determine how much scaffolding to provide, and determine to what extent children may be able to relate to the information presented during instruction. It is also important to understand children's development in other learning strategies.

Metacognition and Cognitive Strategies

Metacognition is the ability to reflect on one's own thought processes and cognitive strategies. Students become increasingly metacognitive throughout middle childhood. Third graders, who are increasingly more metacognitive, can often regulate cognitive processes to maximize learning and memory. They can make decisions about the types of strategies to utilize while reading and determine whether or not they understand what they are reading.

The main learning strategy of third graders tends to be rehearsal, in which students try to learn information and remember what they have learned by repeating it again and again. Most third graders are also beginning to use organization as a learning strategy, that is, looking for relationships among bits of information in order to learn about them. Children in middle childhood tend to think they can remember more than they are actually capable of remembering, however (McDevitt & Ormrod, 2002).

We have briefly discussed cognitive perspectives relevant to literacy instruction. The basic information gleaned from this discussion can help us understand the ways in which our students process information as they learn. It is important to keep these general features of third-grade learners in mind so we are able to plan and implement developmentally appropriate instruction. Next, we will consider the social characteristics of typical third graders.

SOCIAL CHARACTERISTICS OF THIRD GRADERS

As a teacher of third-grade students, you may have certain social expectations for them. You may stress the importance of such things as being polite, being a good friend, or being honest. There may even be a space on the report card for you to communicate to parents how their children act in social situations. Most teachers have certain social expectations for their students for many reasons, such as the teachers' background or the school environment. You may remember when you were in school and how you were always taught to respect your elders. This may be a standard to which you hold your students, stressing its importance on a daily basis.

Teaching students and reinforcing social rules can be a means of managing the classroom and helping students to be well adjusted socially. However, it is important to be aware and respectful of the cultures, backgrounds, and values of the students and their families. The values and beliefs of a teacher are not necessarily those held by students and their families and communities. If a teacher is disrespectful or is unaware of another culture's values, conflict and resistant behaviors may prevail in the classroom. Understanding children's social development can help you set realistic expectations for them.

It is also helpful for teachers to be aware of the developmental social characteristics of their students because the social realm is closely tied to other areas of student development. Developmental psychologists believe that, from birth, a child is embedded in a plethora of social relationships. As the child grows older, these relationships branch out and increase in complexity. "Despite the many differences in the nature and function of relationships, there are reasons to believe that they are not just common to children's experiences but essential for their development" (Kindermann, 2003, p. 408). We will touch upon a few key areas of social development, including social cognition, social competence, and social conventions, so you may gain a general idea of what to expect from your students socially.

Let's begin with social cognition. Social cognition is how students think about people and society, as well as how they think about themselves in society. Third graders' social cognition typically involves focusing on concrete observable features of themselves and others. For instance, when listening to or reading a story or when asked to focus on character traits, students may first recall what the character wore or did rather than his or her emotional state (e.g., friendly or grouchy) or psychological characteristics (e.g., bossy or shallow). As children's social cognition develops, they may address more abstract concepts such as emotions and attitudes (McDevitt & Ormrod, 2002).

Social competence deals with the skills children use to be successful as they function socially with their peers (Cole & Cole, 2001). Under the umbrella of social competence lies the notion of social perspective through which children are able to adopt the perspective of another person. Selman (1981) looked at children's levels of perspective taking and compared them to developmental levels of friendship. In the former, most third graders would fall in level 2 (out of 4), or the self-reflective or reciprocal perspective. Children at this level are able to see differences in their own feelings and thoughts from those of another. In the latter, those in middle childhood fell in stage 2 (out of 4), which was categorized as fair-weather cooperation. In this stage, children are aware that people can have different perspectives. In their relationships, children focus on adjusting their perspectives and cooperating with friends. However, these relationships can be easily destroyed when there is an argument.

I have had talks with many tearful children who felt as if their world had come crashing down around them because they were in a fight with one of their friends. Because of their level of social and cognitive development, most third-grade students have difficulty in seeing the argument as temporary and struggle with how to use skills to alleviate the stressful situation. Teachers should help foster students' positive interactions with peers by designing cooperative learning activities and allowing time for discussion and debriefing of them.

McDevitt and Ormrod (2002) summarized additional social characteristics predominant during middle childhood. Children in this age group have a heightened empathy for people whom they have never met who may be suffering. For instance, most third graders are beginning to be able to put themselves in others' shoes. The students with whom I worked all received free lunches because their families were poor. The school was adopted by a neighboring wealthy, suburban school district, which brought Christmas presents and school supplies to the third graders. The students got to know one another through letters. At one point, the third graders in my school learned that one of their friends from the suburban school had a house fire. Our students raised as much money as they could for the girl and her family. It was as if they were able to feel the great loss she and her family had suffered.

Third graders also have a greater understanding of social conventions for suitable behavior, and they are beginning to see the importance of cooperating and compromising with others. In addition, they tend to feel more guilt and shame when they do something morally wrong (McDevitt & Ormrod, 2002). I was able to see evidence of these social characteristics during circle meetings, peer discussions, and debriefing after peer discussions and other classroom activities. Most of the time my third graders had rules to follow and to enforce among themselves in these situations. They were able to recognize when their classmates were not following the designated rules, and they were regretful when they, themselves, did not do so.

The social characteristics of third graders, or children in middle childhood, should be used as a general framework when planning classroom activities and considering the social expectations we have for our students. We should structure developmentally appropriate activities that allow students to grow socially, with a great deal of support from teachers' modeling and reinforcement.

EMOTIONAL CHARACTERISTICS OF THIRD GRADERS

As we try to get to know our third graders, it is easier for us to gather information about their cognitive and social abilities. We can give them assessments to measure their cognitive abilities, and we can make observations about how they interact socially with their peers and other adults with whom they come into contact during the school day. However, it is difficult to get a handle on some students' emotions. For instance, some children are less verbal and are shy about showing how they are feeling.

The work of Erikson (1963) and the notions of self-concept and self-esteem can foster a general understanding of third graders' emotional characteristics. Erikson's psychosocial theory of development involves a series of stages. Within each stage, it is believed, children face a developmental crisis, and the outcome of that crisis affects later stages. Eight stages lead from birth to adulthood. Children in third grade fall in Erikson's fourth stage, known as industry versus inferiority (Woolfolk, 1998).

Children in third grade are beginning to see that hard work pays off. Woolfolk (1998, p. 69) stated, "They are beginning to see the relationship between perseverance and the pleasure of a job completed. The crisis at this stage is industry versus inferiority." Difficulty with school or making friends may lead to feelings of inferiority. Students who have difficulty with reading early in their school careers may carry these feelings of inferiority into other subject areas and other aspects of their lives. Early intervention, flexible grouping, careful attention to learning styles, and a warm and caring classroom environment may alleviate feelings of inferiority.

Some of my third-grade students become very upset when they receive poor grades or lower grades than their friends. We often have whole-class and individual discussions to talk about these feelings, sometimes focusing on why some students performed better (e.g., because they studied, paid attention in class, or were stronger in one subject than another). One way to help students achieve success is to provide rubrics to make them aware of the expectations for the assignment (see Figure 1.1). The website rubistar.4teachers.org/index.php is useful for producing similar rubrics. This will be expanded upon when we discuss the affective characteristics of third graders.

Understanding notions of self-concept and self-esteem can also help us better comprehend the emotional development of our students. Self-concept deals with students' perceptions of themselves. Self-esteem is the value students place on their own abilities, features, and behaviors (Woolfolk, 1998). Children in middle childhood tend to have a positive self-concept. In general, third graders increasingly base their perceptions of their abilities on how others perform. At this age, they tend to form closer ties with their peers and teachers and are better able to regulate their emotions (McDevitt & Ormrod, 2002). We should keep these general emotional characteristics in mind as we differentiate our instruction according to the needs of our learners. Likewise, these characteristics should be considered when providing motivational incentives to foster literacy growth.

AFFECTIVE CHARACTERISTICS OF THIRD GRADERS

Affective characteristics refer in general to a student's motivation for learning. Piaget saw many parallels between cognitive and affective development among children, particularly at the concrete operations stage. If you recall, this is the

Category	4	3	2	1
Focus on Topic (Content)	There is one clear, well-focused topic. Main idea stands out and is supported by detailed information. Student elaborates beyond grade-level requirements of the task.	Main idea is clear, but the supporting information is general or needs more elaboration.	Main idea is somewhat clear, but there is a need for more supporting information. May contain irrelevant details.	Main idea is not clear. Includes few or no details.
Organization	Organizes content and ideas in a logical way and is fluent and cohesive. Transitions are creative.	Organizes content in a logical way, although transitions may not be fluent.	Attempts to organize content and ideas but is not consistently fluent or omits transitions.	Does not present content in an organized or logical way.
Grammar, Spelling, Mechanics	Few, if any, mistakes in grammar, mechanics, and usage that do not detract from clarity and meaning. Demonstrates above-grade-level knowledge of conventions.	May contain minor errors in grammar, spelling, or mechanics but do not detract from clarity and meaning.	Contains errors in grammar, spelling, or mechanics that interfere with clarity and meaning.	Writing demonstrates minimal control of grammar, spelling, or mechanics, which greatly interfere with clarity and meaning.
Word Choice	Uses precise and vivid words and phrases that draw pictures in the reader's mind. Word choice and placement seem accurate, natural, and not forced.	Uses vivid words and phrases that draw pictures in the reader's mind, but occasionally words are used inaccurately or seem overdone.	Uses words that communicate clearly, but writing lacks variety, impact, or flair.	Uses a limited vocabulary that does not communicate strongly or capture the reader's interest.
Sentence Structure (Sentence Fluency)	Sentences are well-constructed, with varied structure. Writing allows for fluid reading.	Most sentences are well constructed, with varied structure. Writing enables fluid reading.	A few sentences are well constructed but have a similar structure.	Sentences lack structure and appear incomplete or rambling.
Adding Personality (Voice)	Writing is unique and expresses the author's knowledge and experience. Author has taken the ideas and made them "her own."	Seems to draw on knowledge or experience, but there is some lack of ownership of the topic.	Relates some of his own knowledge or experience, but it adds nothing to the discussion of the topic.	Writer has not tried to transform the information in a personal way. Ideas and the way they are expressed seem to belong to someone else.

FIGURE 1.1. Third-grade writing rubric.

Piagetian stage in which we find most third graders. Because children in this stage become cognitively able to differentiate their own perspectives from those of others, reason deductively, and make inferences, these same cognitive tools are available to regulate their affective reasoning—which means they become increasingly better at evaluating arguments rather than simply accepting ideas at face value. As students grow in their ability to evaluate and make judgments about arguments, they are better able to consider the motivation behind a particular statement (Wadsworth, 1984). This means that third graders are beginning to consider the motivations behind their own and others' words and actions. Having developed this ability, third graders are more likely to give critical thought to, and make judgments about, the content learned in school and the instructional activities in which they participate. This means that third graders can begin to think critically about and evaluate what they read and write, but it also means that they are more critical of their own abilities and more aware of their interests. This developmental characteristic may explain a decline in students' attitudes toward reading around third grade (McKenna, Kear, & Ellsworth, 1995). Third grade is the first point at which most students are developmentally able to evaluate their motivation.

In general, motivation is defined as "an internal state that arouses, directs, and maintains behavior" (Woolfolk, 1998, p. 372). As a teacher, I hope all of my students are motivated to learn. When some students are not as excited or interested in learning as others, I think about the cause and what I can do to motivate them.

There are two types of motivation: intrinsic and extrinsic. Students who are intrinsically motivated are driven internally (have desires from within) to complete a task. These students take pride in achievement and perform well for their own pleasure. Students who are extrinsically motivated perform a task for external factors unrelated to the task. For example, these students may try to do well in school because they are being rewarded monetarily by their parents for every good grade.

Woolfolk (1998) suggested four general approaches for motivating students: behavioral, humanistic, cognitive, and social learning. Behaviorists help to explain motivation in terms of rewards and incentives; that is, behaviors consistently reinforced may grow into tendencies or habits. For instance, children who are consistently praised for doing their homework will continue to work hard to complete it. Rewards and punishments for various behaviors foster extrinsic motivation.

The humanistic view of motivation stems from the belief that "people are continually motivated by the inborn need to fulfill their potential" (Woolfolk, 1998, p. 375). This perspective stresses the importance of fostering intrinsic motivation, self-esteem, self-actualization, and autonomy. Teachers can foster this type of motivation by teaching students how to appropriately select books, giving students reading materials that interest them, and allowing them, independently or with peers, to make sense of what they are reading, with appropriate scaffolding.

Those who hold to the cognitive viewpoint of motivation believe that our thinking, rather than rewards and punishments, determines our behaviors. "One of the central assumptions in cognitive approaches is that people respond not to external events or physical conditions like hunger, but rather to their interpretations of these events" (Woolfolk, 1998, p. 377). When individuals rely on internal states (e.g., thought or amount of effort) rather than external events to determine their actions and behaviors, they are better able to control the outcome, which leads to higher levels of self-esteem. In school, it is important to understand how people explain their successes and failures—usually through causal explanations or attributions (McDevitt & Ormrod, 2002)—because these explanations have direct implications for affective development. Weiner (1986) describes three dimensions of attributions: internal versus external, stable versus unstable, and controllable versus uncontrollable.

In the internal versus external dimension, children may see the cause of an event as a product of something within themselves or something outside themselves. For instance, a child's attributions are internal if she believes that she did well on a test because she studied every evening for a week. A child with external attributions may believe he failed a test because the teacher doesn't like him and gave him a bad grade. The stable versus unstable dimension deals with whether children attribute the cause of events to factors that change very little (stable) or factors that tend to vary (unstable). A child who believes that if he studies and works hard, he will do well attributes his success to stable factors (e.g., effort). A child who believes that she has passed a test because of luck is attributing her success to unstable factors. Finally, in the dimension of controllable versus uncontrollable, children attribute events to factors they are able to influence or to factors that they cannot influence (McDevitt & Ormrod, 2002). For example, the decision to study for an exam or put forth effort is controllable. When children attribute their success (or failure) to a controllable factor, their self-esteem is enhanced because they realize they control the outcome. When children attribute their success (or failure) to an uncontrollable factor such as luck or the difficulty of the task, their self-esteem is diminished because they link their success (or failure) to an external factor that is outside of their control. We hope students are internally motivated, believing that events are due to stable factors within their control. When students attribute their success and failure to these factors, their self-esteem is enhanced.

The fourth approach to motivation is social learning, which combines the behavioral and cognitive approaches to motivation (Woolfolk, 1998). This view interprets motivation as the joining of a child's expectation of reaching a goal and how much the child values the goal.

Now that we have a general understanding of some of the perspectives on motivation, we will discuss motivation and what we can expect, in general, from our third graders. For third graders, the ability to delay gratification will increase. You will find in your students a growing awareness of how their own performance compares with the performance of others. Our students will also have a more realistic evaluation of their own abilities to perform. Third graders are better able to see that effort and ability can cause both success and failure. They are also beginning to attribute success to hard work (McDevitt & Ormrod, 2002), which is particularly important in literacy instruction as we begin to teach strategies for recognizing words and comprehending text. Using strategies requires time, effort, and persistence. If students are capable of attributing successful word recognition and comprehension to the amount of effort they invested, their self-esteem as readers will be enhanced, they will become more positive about reading, and they will be more likely to persist in their efforts.

Motivation can have a huge impact on our literacy instruction and student performance. Specific methods to assess student motivation will be discussed in Chapter 4. Knowing how motivated our students are may lead us to alternative types of instruction, more varied texts, or other means of getting students excited about learning in order to increase achievement.

SUMMARY

Having a deeper understanding of the cognitive, social, emotional, and affective characteristics of third graders can give us a better idea of what to expect from our students so that we can plan developmentally appropriate instruction.

Some of the major perspectives in cognitive development, such as the views of Piaget, Vygotsky, and the information-processing view were explained, as was metacognition. In sum, children are viewed as active learners, and learning takes place in a social context. Cognitive development could be fostered by adults or more knowledgeable peers who help them perform challenging activities successfully. Third graders are beginning to be able to think about their own thought processes; however they are still, for the most part, concrete learners.

Third graders tend to cooperate more in relationships. They are increasingly more empathetic and see the importance of social conventions. They recognize the social qualities of others but tend to focus more on concrete features.

Emotional characteristics of third graders include, in general, a positive self-concept. They begin to form closer ties with peers and teachers and tend to compare their own abilities to the performance of their classmates. Third graders are increasingly able to regulate their emotions and to see that hard work can pay off.

As we consider our students' affective characteristics, we can keep in mind the four approaches to motivation: behavioral, humanistic, cognitive, and social learning. For third graders, success is increasingly attributed to hard work. They are also beginning to make more realistic evaluations of their own abilities.

CHAPTER 2

WHAT ARE APPROPRIATE GOALS FOR LITERACY LEARNERS IN THIRD GRADE?

I t is not easy to be a teacher of literacy because there is so much to consider. First, teachers must decide what literacy means to them. Then, they must realize that their definition of literacy may not match the students', the school's, or the state's ideas about literacy. Teachers must consider all of these views as they plan and implement instruction.

Most U.S. states have adopted English Language Arts (ELA) standards, with which the states expect teachers' curricula and instruction to be aligned. Many states are also giving increasingly more state assessments to measure students' achievement of the skills outlined in the standards. As a consequence, such standards and assessments must also be considered by literacy teachers. Most states have websites for teachers to download the standards. There is also a set of national standards for the ELA sponsored by the National Council of Teachers of English and the International Reading Association (www.ncte.org/about/over/standards/110846.htm).

Along with your notions of literacy and those of your school and state, you also must consider the needs of your students. Not all of your third graders will be reading and writing at a third-grade level. Some students will be well below grade level, and others will be well above. However, it is important to have appropriate expectations for your students, so you can meet them at their point of need and facilitate their growth to the highest possible level. In this chapter we will outline what you can expect, in general, from your third graders in specific areas of literacy.

Third graders are reading and writing at all different levels. Some students may have appropriate word identification skills but need work with comprehension. Others may have adequate word identification and comprehension skills but be unmotivated. Your learners will vary greatly, and it will be important for you to consider their individual needs when planning instruction. The information in this chapter will give you an overall sense of what to expect from your third graders, as well as some general goals for their instruction.

WHAT ARE A THIRD GRADER'S WORD IDENTIFICATION SKILLS LIKE?

Word identification skills are what students use to figure out the words they are reading. We may also call this decoding, text recognition, word attack, or word identification. Most third graders will already have some word identification skills: sound phonemic awareness, a well-developed sight vocabulary, and an understanding of letter-sound relationships. Sight vocabulary refers to those words students can recognize immediately and automatically. When planning for your third graders' instruction, it is important to understand, in general, how children learn to read words.

Phases of Learning to Read Words

Ehri (1991) described four phases in learning to read words: the logographic phase, the transitional phase (logographic/alphabetic), the alphabetic phase, and the orthographic phase. Early readers tend to be characterized as logographic readers. Children in this phase read words by using graphic features. For example, they might use the shape or the length of the word as features to help them identify the word. The transitional phase is used to describe readers who are on the fringes of the logographic and alphabetic phases. Students who are in the alphabetic phase use the relations between graphemes and phonemes to read words. This leads to the orthographic phase, where we hope to see most of our third graders.

Orthographic readers are able to figure out unknown words by analogizing to known words and by chunking polysyllabic words into smaller units. That is, orthographic readers reorganize smaller parts within large words and blend the parts together. No longer do these readers have to sound out every single letter in a word to figure out what it is. They can look at an unknown word and liken it to a word they do know. For instance, a child may not know the word *handstand*. He may say to himself:

> "This is a long word that I don't know, but part of the word looks like a word I do know. Both *hand* and *stand* look like the word *sand*. I see the word *and* in this word twice. All I have to do is change the beginning sounds to fig-

ure out this long word I don't know. I will blend together the beginning sound with the word I know (*h* + *and*) and say the word *hand*. That makes sense. Now I will try the second part of the word. I will blend the *s* and the *t* and put that with *and* to make *stand*. Then I will put the words together to see if they make sense. The word is *handstand*. That makes sense. I know what a handstand is and it fits right in with the story I am reading."

Children in the orthographic phase are also able to identify word parts, such as prefixes and suffixes, to figure out unknown words. They can break apart or chunk large words to make the parts more manageable without having to figure out every letter sound. For example, a child may come to the word *disrespectfully*. Instead of first sounding out the *d-i-s-r-e-s-p-e-c-t-f-u-l-l-y*, the child may say to herself:

"I see the prefixes *dis* and *re*. I also see the endings *ful* and *ly*. I just have to sound out the *spect* and put them altogether (*dis-re-spect-ful-ly*). That makes sense."

Because the child does not have to sound out every single letter, her reading speed increases (Almasi, 2003; Ehri, 1991). Bear, Invernizzi, Templeton, and Johnston (2000) also outlined reading and spelling stages. According to their work, third graders should be at the intermediate stage, which focuses on syllables and affixes.

Intermediate readers are able to automatically identify consonant and vowel patterns in monosyllabic words, which act as scaffolds in their reading of polysyllabic words. Intermediate readers are learning to identify the known consonant and vowel patterns in polysyllabic words and study syllables more carefully. "They are also developing a more efficient word identification routine for reading, because the ability to perceive syllables rapidly within polysyllabic words contributes to reading efficiently" (Bear et al., 2000, p. 221).

Again, it is our hope that our third graders are orthographic readers, or intermediate readers, but you may find that your students are moving in and out of the various phases.

Appropriate Goals for Word Identification Instruction

Having knowledge of third graders' word identification skills can help you set goals for your students. Third graders should possess a variety of strategies to figure out unknown words (Almasi, 2003). The strategies you will need to teach your students may vary. Also, some students may be familiar with certain decoding strategies but not yet able to use them independently and across different reading situations.

As a third-grade teacher, I (KG-Y) had different groups during the guided reading portion of the day. These groups changed according to the needs of the students and their reading levels. I was beginning to teach one group how to analogize to known words, and I was fostering another group's independent use of the same strategy.

Assessments will need to be administered to determine what word identification goals are appropriate for each student (such assessments will be discussed in more detail in Chapter 4). A teacher must meet the students at the level at which they are reading and make every attempt to help them grow as readers during the school year. In one class, my students' reading levels ranged from a preprimer to a fourth-grade level. Some of my students were working on sight words and phonics, while others were able to analogize to known words and chunk words as a means of decoding polysyllabic words.

In general, third graders should know that words can be divided into small and large sound units. They should also know that "the same multisound units are part of many different words, as the 'ter' in 'butter' and 'terrific' " (Fox, 2000, p. 143). Students should be able to blend together sound units, as well as individual sounds, to figure out a word. Using this type of "multiletter chunk" strategy requires less mental attention for figuring out unknown words and provides more time and energy for students to focus on understanding what they are reading.

Third graders, in general, should also be able to correct any words they did not chunk or figure out correctly. Fox (2000, p. 144) offers the following options for students if a word is incorrectly identified:

1. Rechunk (divide words into different multiletter groups and then reblend).

2. Fall back on either the letter-sound or analogy strategy.

3. Look up words in the dictionary.

4. Ask expert readers for help.

When you are working with third graders who are on grade level as far as their word identification skills are concerned, you will focus on prefixes, suffixes, root words, compound words, contractions, and various syllable and accent patterns to foster students' knowledge and use of the chunking strategy (Fox, 2000).

Bear et al. (2000, p. 221) have outlined a sequence for teaching the elements associated with the chunking strategy: "A sequence of teaching about structural elements should be followed: syllables, affixes, and the effects of affixes on the base words to which they are attached." Teaching the concepts of open and closed syllables, accents, vowel patterns, base words (root words), prefixes, and suffixes as part of word study will enhance the use and understanding of the chunking strategy and also assist with spelling.

In their book *Words Their Way*, Bear et al. (2000) include a specific outline of instruction at the intermediate reader stage that begins with plural endings and concludes with base words and simple suffixes. They also include many activities that can be used in the classroom for student practice during word study or guided reading groups.

Remember that you will not necessarily be teaching this skill to all of your students because some of them may not be ready for this strategy at the same time. Some students will arrive in third grade at an alphabetic phase, in which they are still trying to read polysyllabic words one letter at a time. To help move these students to an orthographic phase, or help them to become intermediate readers, you will need to begin teaching them that larger words can be broken down into smaller parts and that they should first read the "chunkable" words. Then you will need to help them learn to look inside large words for smaller chunks and teach them how to blend the chunks together.

Knowledge of Ehri's (1991) phases of learning and characteristics of intermediate readers, coupled with your observations and assessments, will be helpful in determining individual goals for your students' growth in word identification skills. It is also important to align your instruction with the ELA learning standards of your state. These standards may require instruction or proficiency in the use of word identification strategies in various types of texts or in certain learning situations. It is crucial that we provide solid instruction of word identification skills so that students are able to pay closer attention to understanding what they are reading rather than figuring out all of the words. Another aspect of reading, fluency, can also have an impact on how students focus on understanding what they are reading.

WHAT IS A THIRD GRADER'S FLUENCY LIKE?

Griffith and Rasinski (2004, p. 126) define fluency as "the ability to read accurately, quickly, effortlessly, and with appropriate expression and meaning." Because fluent readers can spend less effort on decoding text, they are able to focus more on comprehension. Because of the limited amount of attention individuals can expend on reading (LaBerge & Samuels, 1974), if too much cognitive effort is spent on decoding words in a text, attention is taken away from comprehension.

Students typically become fluent readers in second grade (Kuhn & Stahl, 2003; Chall, 1996; Rasinski, Padak, Linek, & Sturtevant, 1994). Therefore, as third-grade teachers, we hope most of our students will be able to read fluently. However, as with word identification skills, we will most likely have students in class who are not yet reading fluently.

Appropriate Goals for Fluency Instruction

Hudson, Lane, and Pullen (2005) recommend that, when reading texts at an independent level, third graders should be reading 79 correct words per minute in the fall, 84–93 correct words per minute in the winter, and 100–114 correct words per minute in the spring. Similarly, Rasinski and Padak (1996) believe that third graders should be reading about 110 words per minute. These will be helpful guidelines as you assess your students' reading fluency (more information related to assessing fluency will be found in Chapter 4). Students who struggle to meet these fluency guidelines should be working to improve their correct words per minute by one to three words a week (Hudson et al., 2005).

Worthy and Broaddus (2002) recommend reading performance as one method of fluency instruction and practice. Reading performance requires students to rehearse a text while the teacher provides instruction and feedback. As will be discussed further in Chapter 3, third graders still like to gather around the teacher to listen to texts. Reading aloud to your students will give them a good example of fluent oral reading, which includes reading at an appropriate rate, reading smoothly, and reading with expression. You should also provide instruction about factors that enhance fluency (e.g., appropriate rate, smoothness, and expression). After modeling and giving instruction, you will need to provide opportunities for guided practice and independent practice, using a wide range of texts.

Opitz and Rasinski (1998) recommend a plethora of activities to improve oral reading fluency, such as revised radio reading, shared book experience, choral reading, mentor reading, and Readers' Theater. In *revised radio reading*, students rehearse and perform portions of text. One student is the radio announcer (reader), and the rest are listeners in the same way one might listen to a story on the radio. At the end of the section of text, the reader leads a discussion about what was read.

In *shared book experience*, often used with students in grades K–2, as well as with older students, the teacher reads the book aloud and students interact with her and each other as the book is read. For example, students may chorally chant repetitious words or phrases. Through this experience, students can learn how to analyze words and understand what is being read.

In *choral reading*, all students read with the teacher in unison. This helps students learn to read at an appropriate rate. The students' self-esteem is preserved because they do not have to read aloud by themselves. Uncertain children's voices can blend in with other voices to chant those parts they know well.

Mentor reading takes place between two individuals. The mentor can be a teacher, other adult, or a more knowledgeable student. The mentor offers support to the student who is reading the text. Finally, *Readers' Theater* allows groups of students to read from a script for an audience after rehearsal. The goal is to read smoothly and with expression. In my (KG-Y) third-grade classroom, Readers' Theater works particularly well. Scripts can be made from any text students are reading. I simply took stories they were required to read from the mandated reading series and turned them into scripts. This is a way to make a third-grade text accessible to students who are not yet reading at a third-grade level. You can differentiate instruction by tailoring various parts in a script to specific students, depending on ability or interest. After assigning parts, students should have multiple opportunities to rehearse the parts by reading from the script. Students should be allowed to use the script at all times, even during the final performance. The performance centers around reading smoothly and with expression, not on memorizing lines, props, or actions. Performances can take place informally in small groups, in front of the classroom, or on a stage. Readers' Theater can be very motivating for third graders and can improve fluency. More information related to fluency instruction and assessment is found in Chapters 3 and 4.

WHAT IS A THIRD GRADER'S COMPREHENSION LIKE?

As we have already discussed, in general a third-grade reader should be spending less time on decoding words (as it should be more automatic) and more on understanding what he or she is reading. Comprehension relates to the ability to understand what is read. Third grade is an important year in which to help build students' comprehension strategies and skills (Snow, Burns, & Griffin, 1998).

Just as readers need a variety of word identification strategies, they also need a variety of comprehension strategies. Almasi (2003) divided comprehension strategies into three groups: text anticipation, text maintenance, and fix-up strategies.

Text Anticipation Strategies

Text anticipation strategies involve accessing prior knowledge. They include previewing a text; activating relevant background knowledge; setting purposes for reading; generating, maintaining, and revising predictions; and identifying text structure (Almasi, 2003). With these strategies, your third graders will have more options available to them as they read.

The ability to *preview text* is important. Examining the title, pictures, contents, and other features of a text allows students to get an idea of what the text is about, which helps them *identify text structure*. If a student notices headings, subheadings, words in boldface type, charts, graphs, and an index while previewing a text, she can surmise that it is an expository text. She knows she will be finding out information about a topic. If a student notices characters and setting while previewing the text, he can prepare to read a narrative text or a story. Third graders tend to be more familiar with narrative text structure with expository text structure because of all the bedtime stories and read-alouds they've experienced. It is important for third graders to know the difference between the two kinds of texts and their features.

Previewing a text also allows students to *activate their prior knowledge*, or tap into their background knowledge, about the topic of the text they will be reading. Students should think about what they already know about the title or topic, which helps them make connections between what they already know and what they will learn. It also gives them a place to attach new information they may glean from the text.

Previewing a text can also help students with another strategy, to *set their own purposes* for reading. Tompkins and McGee (1992) describe ways in which teachers can help students set purposes for reading a text, such as using K-W-L charts

(Ogle, 1986) and self-questioning techniques. This strategy should be taught explicitly to students by using a great deal of modeling. Students should be given guided practice and shown how to set purposes for different kinds of texts, the goal being independence.

Finally, previewing a text can help students to *make predictions* about the text they are about to read or are reading, which helps to focus their attention (Almasi, 2003). Third graders should be able to generate, verify, and revise predictions before and while they read in order to foster comprehension.

Text Maintenance Strategies

Text maintenance can become overwhelming for students because the amount of text they are expected to read increases rapidly in third grade. Thus, you will need to support the development of text maintenance strategies, which keep readers focused and include creating mental images, questioning oneself for the purpose of monitoring comprehension, identifying text structure, and revising predictions (Almasi, 2003).

Creating mental pictures, or visualizing, helps to focus students' attention while reading. Moreover, as Harvey and Goudvis (2000, p. 97) state, "Visualizing brings joy to reading. When we visualize, we create pictures in our minds that belong to us and no one else." Students are more likely to remember and understand what they are reading if they are able to create pictures in their minds (Almasi, 2003).

Questioning oneself is an important strategy for third graders. Questioning is the key to understanding because questions can help clarify any confusions students may have and also allow for a deeper understanding of the text. "When our students ask questions and search for answers, we know that they are monitoring comprehension and interacting with the text to construct meaning, which is exactly what we hope for developing readers (Harvey & Goudvis, 2000, p. 82).

As students become more familiar with the features of narrative and expository texts, as discussed previously, they will benefit from learning more about the specific types of text structures. For instance, students should be familiar with the five main types of expository structure (description, sequence, comparison, cause and effect, and problem–solution). Third graders can use cue words in the text to identify text structure and deepen their understanding.

Students should learn to *update their predictions* as they read, which helps to foster comprehension. Creating mental images, questioning oneself, identifying text structure, and revising predictions all help students to focus their attention while reading (Almasi, 2003).

Fix-Up Strategies

Rereading, slowing down, reading ahead for clarification, and discussing trouble spots with others are all fix-up strategies. Good readers use these strategies when they come to the realization that they do not understand what they are reading. "They may stop and reread more slowly, or they may just continue to read knowing that sometimes confusions are clarified by information presented later in the text" (Tompkins & McGee, 1992, p. 261). Discussing confusing portions of texts with a partner, peers in a small group, or an adult can also be used to deepen comprehension.

Text anticipation, text maintenance, and fix-up strategies can be used flexibly and in combination with one another. Third graders should be able to use several of these strategies independently by the end of the school year. Almasi (2003) explains these comprehension strategies more fully.

Appropriate Goals for Comprehension Instruction

Asking children a couple of comprehension questions after they have read something will not foster comprehension skill or strategy use. Students need explicit instruction, modeling, and guided practice on *what* the strategies are, *how* they are used, and *when and why* students should use them. Teachers should also provide students with the appropriate amount of scaffolding to ease them into the independent use of a variety of comprehension strategies in a range of texts (Almasi, 2003). The instructional goals you have for your third graders should help foster growth of comprehension strategies through explicit instruction, modeling, and guided practice. This instruction should occur while using a wide range of texts in which students can practice using the strategies they are learning.

Although all students will not be functioning at the same level, Snow et al. (1998, p. 83) believe that third-grade readers should be able to

- ➢ Read aloud with fluency and comprehension any text that is appropriately designed for a third-grade level.
- ➢ Read and comprehend both fiction and nonfiction that is appropriately designed for the third-grade level.
- ➢ Summarize major points from fiction and nonfiction texts.
- ➢ Ask how, why, and what-if questions in interpreting nonfiction texts.
- ➢ In interpreting nonfiction, distinguish cause and effect, fact and opinion, and main idea and supporting details.

Various teaching methods and tools can be used as part of comprehension strategy instruction. It may be helpful to keep these in mind as you examine the instructional goals of your third graders. Almasi (2003) offers detailed descriptions of how these methods can be used, as well as sample lesson plans.

One teaching tool for comprehension strategies is the K-W-L chart (Ogle, 1986). This procedure can help activate prior knowledge and set purposes for reading. Picture walks and rich discussions help children with previewing text. Story maps and graphic organizers help students with the identification of text structure. Directed reading–thinking activities (DR–TA) and journaling can help teach students to make predictions.

In my classroom, comprehension instruction took place throughout the day. For instance, some students were learning how to make predictions while watching a cartoon clip during a flexible group time; other students were practicing making predictions independently by writing them on sticky notes and then revising or confirming them as they continued to read. The process involved in making predictions was visited throughout the day by relating it to estimation in math and forming hypotheses in science. We made predictions as a whole group during shared reading and during read-alouds.

Teachers must help students develop their comprehension skills and strategies by revealing their own thought processes. Through these think-alouds, we can let our students see how we understand text and the questions and ideas we have about what we are reading. We should refrain from asking literal comprehension questions as our sole means of touching upon comprehension in the classroom. We must teach our third graders the skills and strategies they need to understand texts on their own.

WHAT IS A THIRD GRADER'S VOCABULARY LIKE?

Vocabulary refers to knowing and understanding word meanings. It is considered one of the best predictors of reading achievement and plays a large role in comprehension (Daneman, 1991). For students to understand what they are reading, they must know the meanings of key words in the text. Third graders should be rapidly building their vocabularies each day. In third grade, content area texts become more complex, and students will need to know the meanings of key terms in order to understand, for example, the process of photosynthesis or customs of people in other countries.

Although not all third graders will be at the same level in vocabulary development, we can look at some of its general characteristics to get an idea of where they are. Your third-grade students should be able to determine the meanings of words from context (contextual analysis). For instance, they should be able to use the words and pictures surrounding the unknown word to help discern its meaning. They should also be able to look at word parts (root words, prefixes, and suffixes) and use their knowledge of grammar (e.g., nouns, verbs, and adjectives) to help them determine the meaning (morphemic or structural analysis). Third graders should also begin to consider a word's origin (e.g., Latin or Greek) and its relationship with other words. Through their increasing familiarity with contextual and morphemic analysis, third graders begin to develop strategies for determining the meanings of words independently.

Third graders should also be learning new vocabulary through independent reading and listening to texts read aloud (Edwards, Font, Baumann, & Boland, 2004; Marzano, 2004). Marzano recommended encouraging students to identify and record unknown words of interest to them as they read. In this way, students develop word consciousness and begin to learn strategies for learning meanings independently.

Working independently, however, should not include looking up lists of words in the dictionary. Having students locate and write definitions of words does not foster long-term retention. Scott and Nagy (1989) found that students frequently use one or two words from a definition in the dictionary as the entire meaning of the word. Beck, McKeown, and Kucan (2002) suggest defining words in context and developing student-friendly explanations of their meanings. For example, as teachers are reading aloud, they may come across a word with which their students are not familiar. They can talk about this word within the context of the text. Teachers should explain the meanings of the words by using language students can understand, and they should characterize the word and how it is usually used.

Very often students who need to develop their vocabulary the most are often not the students who are voracious readers. Thus, teachers must find a way to supplement their vocabulary development (Beck et al., 2002). The following section lists specific goals for a more direct approach to teaching specific vocabulary, vocabulary learning strategies, and vocabulary through word consciousness and word play.

Appropriate Goals for Vocabulary Instruction

In their edited volume entitled *Vocabulary Instruction: Research to Practice*, Baumann and Kame'enui (2004) describe three essential parts of vocabulary instruction: (1) teaching specific vocabulary, (2) teaching vocabulary-learning strategies, and (3) teaching vocabulary through word consciousness and language play. Vocabulary development will be enhanced in your third-grade classroom by incorporating these goals into your literacy program.

Teaching Specific Vocabulary

For students to better understand what they are reading across all content areas, they need to work on building their vocabulary. Many of us introduce new vocabulary words as we introduce new texts or new units of study in reading, math, science, social studies, and so on. Students must be taught specific ways to gain an understanding of these new words and to add them to their vocabulary. McKeown and Beck (2004) remind us that it would be impossible to teach students all the words they will need as they read. However, they recommend considering each reader's vocabulary as comprising three tiers. The first tier contains basic words that do not need instructional attention (words like *family, desk, cup,* and *rain*). The third tier consists of words that do not appear frequently and are often specific to certain content areas and domains (e.g., *photosynthesis, hypotenuse, expatriate,* and *butte*). McKeown and Beck suggest that spending large amounts of classroom time to develop rich understandings of third-tier words will not be beneficial for most students. Instead, they recommend teaching these words when needed during a specific lesson (e.g., teaching the term *photosynthesis* during a science lesson).

Second-tier words are those that occur with high frequency across many domains (McKeown & Beck, 2004). To grow as language users and to enhance verbal functioning, students need direct instruction for second-tier words. Beck et al. (2002, p. 17) identify sample second-tier words, such as *merchant, required, maintain, fortunate,* and *benevolent,* and explain how to identify and select them for instruction from the texts in your classroom.

McKeown and Beck (2004) believe that for vocabulary instruction to have a positive impact on comprehension, it should (1) enable students to have multiple exposures to the words being taught, (2) go beyond providing definitions and involve breadth of information, and (3) include deep processing by asking students to think and interact actively with words. One way we can help students learn new words is to embed them in rich semantic descriptions. In their book *Bringing Words to Life: Robust Vocabulary Instruction,* Beck et al. (2002) and, in their chapter, McKeown and Beck (2004) describe many classroom activities deigned to help children compare and contrast words or contexts. McKeown and Beck remind us that rich vocabulary instruction should be open-ended, with the primary goal of provoking thought and active involvement with words.

Beck et al. (2002) also provide a number of activities—such as Word Associations; Have You Ever . . . ?, Applause, Applause; and Idea Completions—that encourage students to work with word meanings. In *Word Associations* students are given new vocabulary words and asked to associate or match the word with a closely related phrase or object. Then they are asked to tell why they made that association. In the activity *Have You Ever . . .* students are asked "if they have ever," and then the vocabulary word is inserted. This allows students to connect the vocabulary word(s) with their own experiences. *Applause, Applause* has students rate by clapping how much they would like a specific vocabulary word to be explained. The more students clap, the more explanation they desire. Then students are asked to explain their ratings. Finally, *Idea Completions* consists of sentence stems containing the vocabulary words. The students have to complete the sentence stems, which are written so that the students really have to think about the meaning of the words when writing their responses. Some of these activities will be described further when we discuss how to assess vocabulary in Chapter 4.

Teaching Vocabulary-Learning Strategies

Because words in the English language are often made up of similar word parts (root words, prefixes, and suffixes), teaching your third graders about word parts and how to use their knowledge of them to make inferences about unknown words can foster vocabulary growth (Baumann & Kame'enui, 2004; Edwards et al.,

2004). This instruction is sometimes referred to as *morphemic analysis* or *structural analysis*.

Graves (2004) has noted that prefixes are particularly valuable to teach because they appear in a large number of words, are relatively few in number, tend to be spelled consistently, and appear at the beginning of words. In general, prefixes appear less frequently in grade 3 texts than in those read typically in grades 4–6. However, when words with prefixes do appear in the texts your third graders are reading, you should give explicit instruction on those that occur most frequently (*un-*, *re-*, *in-*, and *dis-*). Graves provides an excellent 4-day sequence of lessons designed to teach students how to use their knowledge of prefixes to strategically identify unknown words.

Edwards et al. (2004) note that instruction in morphemic analysis (instruction aimed at helping students determine the meaning of words by analyzing meaningful parts such as root words, prefixes, and suffixes) should consist of a sequence in which students learn to disassemble words into their component parts, determine the meanings of the root words and affixes, and then reassemble the parts to determine the meaning of the entire word. When students learn to analyze morphemes, they quickly gain access to the meanings of all words containing similar roots, prefixes, and suffixes. Thus, vocabulary can grow more quickly with morphemic analysis than with instruction in individual word meanings.

Edwards et al. (2004) offer four additional guidelines for instruction in morphemic analysis: (1) provide explicit instruction in how morphemic analysis works, (2) use word families to promote vocabulary growth, (3) promote independent use of morphemic analysis, and (4) remind students that morphemic analysis does not always work. Explicit instruction should include explanation and modeling related to how to look for meaningful word parts in larger words, how to disassemble words into their component parts, how to unlock the meaning of each component part, and how to reassemble the component parts.

To help students gain access to more words, instruction can also be organized by linking words with common roots (word families). For example, the words *retract*, *detract*, *distract*, *attract*, *contract*, *extract*, and *protract* all contain the common Latin root *tract*, meaning to pull, drag, or draw. Clustering instruction around a family of words containing the same root word and teaching students to examine how various prefixes and suffixes alter each word's meaning increase the breadth and depth of students' vocabulary knowledge. The website www.infoplease.com/ipa/A0907036.html contains reference material about Latin roots, prefixes, and suffixes to assist you in determining clusters of words for such instruction.

Because the number of root words, prefixes, and suffixes is vast, Edwards et al. (2004) also remind us that direct instruction related to every morpheme is not only impossible but also impractical. Therefore, it is essential for instruction to focus on how to use morphemic analysis as a strategy students can use independently. Encouraging students to keep a word study notebook—in which they record the unknown word, disassemble it into component parts, identify the meanings of the parts, and identify the strategies they used to make sense of it—is one way to foster independence. Another way is to create "affix" walls in your classroom (similar to a word wall) in which students post together words with common roots, prefixes, or suffixes. These clusters of words can be gathered from students' independent reading and can serve as a basis for future instruction.

Any strategy instruction must alert students to the possibility that it will not work for all words. White, Sowell, and Yanagihara (as cited in Edwards et al., 2004) remind us that some prefixes do not have the same meaning in all words, which can lead students to false meanings. Also, when some prefixes are removed, there is no meaningful root word left to facilitate meaning construction. Finally, when students consider word part clues, they can be misled about the word's true meaning when they reassemble the meaning of each part. That is, at times the meanings of each part do not combine to form a coherent meaning.

Teaching Vocabulary through Word Consciousness and Language/Word Play

Beyond explicit instruction, vocabulary learning can also be fostered in more indirect, or incidental, ways. Blachowicz and Fisher (2004) have suggested that students can become more aware of words by engaging in language play in the classroom. Language play can certainly be planned, but it does not involve explicit instruction related to word meanings. Rather, it involves puns, riddles, and games that encourage students to use what they know about word meanings and apply them in "fun" contexts. These contexts are used to create a word-rich environment in the classroom in which a variety of literacy materials are present, including books, magazines, newspapers, Web-based materials, and games and activities that encourage word play and develop word consciousness. Blachowicz and Fisher suggest such games as word bingo (words are on the bingo card, and the caller calls out definitions), crosswords, jumbles, and commercial games (e.g., Scrabble, Pictionary, Pictionary Junior, Boggle, Scattergories, Outburst, and Outburst Junior).

Word play can become a planned part of your day, but it can also be incorporated throughout the day at opportune moments. You might have students work together to solve riddles or jokes during your literacy block, or you might share riddles or jokes with students before lunch or recess and have them ponder the solutions with their friends. Afterward, various solutions can be discussed. Your riddles and jokes can be random or thematic. For example, if you were developing a science unit on birds, you might use riddles: What kind of bird is always sad? (a bluebird) or What does a duck eat with its soup? (quackers). You can also find time throughout units to teach students how to write their own riddles, jokes, or puns related to your theme. Blachowicz and Fisher (2004) have noted that students can be taught how to create riddles by metacognitively manipulating definitions and word parts. For example, if you were studying chickens, you might have students list different words associated with chickens such as *hen, rooster, peck, crow, chick*, and *fowl*. Select one of the words, say, *hen*, and remove the initial consonant sound /h/, leaving the *-en*. Think of words beginning with *en-*, such as *envelope, entertain, enter,* and *encyclopedia*. Then put the initial consonant sound /h/ onto the beginning of each word to get *henvelope, hentertain, henter,* and *hencyclopedia*. Students can then use these words to make riddles: How does a chicken mail a letter? (in a hen-velope) or What is a chicken's favorite book? (the hencyclopedia). Blachowicz and Fisher suggest that your instruction include modeling, think-alouds related to the thought processes used in creating riddles, and guided practice in which small groups work to create their own riddles; eventually students can write their own riddles independently.

Blachowicz and Fisher (2004) note four principles of word play:

1. Word play is motivating for students.
2. Word play requires students to be metacognitive as they reflect on words, word parts, and context.
3. Word play, when done well, requires students to be active participants as they construct meaning in social settings.
4. Word play helps students learn to see connections and semantic relationships.

When students enjoy the learning process, they are apt to be more motivated and engaged (Blachowicz & Fisher, 2004). Therefore, by developing a word-rich environment that fosters word consciousness in a pleasurable, unimposing, and even amusing way, we enhance the likelihood that word learning will be motivating.

Metacognition is enhanced when students are actively involved in the learning process. That is, rather than merely learning the meanings of words, students must actively "reflect on, manipulate, combine, and recombine the components of words" (Blachowicz & Fisher, 2004, p. 222) to learn vocabulary. Phonological awareness (the ability to segment speech sounds), morphological awareness (awareness of word parts and their meanings), and syntactic awareness (awareness of how words function grammatically in language) are critical to word learning.

Blachowicz and Fisher (2004, p. 222) also remind us that "talk is critical to word play and word learning." Therefore, our classrooms and lessons must encourage students to work together and talk with one another to foster word learning. Although the games mentioned above encourage students to play together and to engage in word play, these games are competitive and do not necessarily foster collaboration. To foster socially constructed meaning, your classroom activities must permit students to think and talk with one another to solve problems. By simply encouraging small groups of students to work as a team (rather than playing individually), word play becomes a socially constructed event.

Finally, Blachowicz and Fisher (2004) suggest that word play helps students learn to see connections between words. Activities in which students work to group words into clusters or sets and label them, construct charts/maps depicting relationships between words, and create webs are all examples of ways in which the semantic relationship between words is fostered. Simply constructing such maps is not sufficient to facilitate word learning. Discussion must accompany these activities so students can talk about why they grouped words together as they did; this helps all students learn to think in new ways and to be flexible in their approach to learning.

WHAT IS A THIRD GRADER'S MOTIVATION FOR LITERACY LIKE?

The children in your classroom will have varying levels of motivation for literacy, depending on the type of activity and text. For instance, most third graders have more positive attitudes toward reading for fun than they do toward academic reading (McKenna & Kear, 1990). However, as noted in Chapter 1, motivation tends to wane with age. Thus, as we plan our instruction, we must consider ways in which we can enhance motivation.

The actual daily tasks teachers have students perform in the classroom are the most reliable indicator of motivation. Teachers should provide students with challenging, open-ended tasks, choices, control over learning, and opportunities for collaboration during reading and writing (Turner & Paris, 1995). However, teachers should be sure that the tasks are not so difficult that they lead to frustration, which has been shown to stifle motivation. "Although most children begin school with positive attitudes and expectations for success, by the end of the primary grades, and increasingly thereafter, some children become disaffected. Difficulties mastering sound–letter relationships or comprehension skills can easily stifle motivation, which can in turn hamper instructional efforts" (Snow et al., 1998, p. 316).

We should also consider our students' opinions, feelings, and choices, as readers are motivated by different factors (Cole, 2002). Thus, we must plan for the diverse interests and motivations of our students in the texts we use, the tasks we require, and the choices we provide.

Appropriate Goals for Student Motivation

Motivation should be an important part of reading instruction, as research has linked motivation with achievement (Gambrell, Palmer, Codling, & Mazzoni, 1996). The first step is to learn about the types of readers you have in your class and what their interests are. I (KG-Y) use the information from interest surveys and initial discussions with my students to set motivational goals for the year (see

Figure 2.1). You can use their responses to determine whether you have reluctant or voracious readers in your class. Their responses will also help you select the texts you make available in the classroom. We will discuss ways to assess motivation in more detail in Chapter 4.

The second step is to make the classroom environment a motivating factor for literacy. To accomplish this, I have set up a large area filled with books and comfortable spaces for reading. The books are organized by genre and topic so students are able to locate quickly and easily the types of books in which they are interested. The books are coded with colored stickers so the students are able to easily return the books they have read. I also vary the levels of books within the genres and topic areas so they are accessible to the different readers in my classroom. I visit library book sales for inexpensive used books that suit the interests of my students. I also borrow collections of books on various topics from the public libraries and set up small areas in the classroom to showcase the books and allow for easy perusal. Whenever I visit a book sale or buy new books, I bring them to school and introduce them to the students. It is important to rotate the books in your classroom library or students will get bored with the limited choices. A way to expand choices in book selection is to set up a book swap. A small area of your school or classroom can house used and unwanted books brought in by students, who will exchange them for the unwanted books of others.

The third step is to teach students to appropriately select texts. If children are selecting inappropriate books, they may become frustrated. Students can be taught the five-finger method to help them learn to select appropriate books for their developmental level (see Figure 2.2). It is a good idea to model how to select a book from the shelf. Show how to page through the book, selecting one page from the middle of the book and reading it yourself. As you read, count on your fingers the number of words you do not know. If you have five fingers up by the time you reach the bottom of the page, the book may be too difficult. If you have no fingers up, the book may be too easy. When you teach children how to find books that are just right for them, they are more likely to have a motivating reading experience.

A final step is to vary the types of instructional methods and activities in your classroom. My third graders are particularly motivated by peer discussions. They enjoy talking with their friends about common books they are reading. They also enjoy working with one another to figure out confusing parts of the book.

Another extremely motivating activity, especially for my reluctant readers, is book buddies. At the beginning of the school year, I make arrangements with either a kindergarten or first-grade class and match each of my students with a younger book buddy. My third graders read the first-grade texts with their buddies or select other rehearsed texts to read to their first-grade friends. I have found this to be a very empowering and positive experience for most third graders. Whereas these steps may give you some initial ideas, your goals will vary from year to year as the interests and "reading personalities" of your students change (Cole, 2002).

1. How old are you? _____

2. What do you do for fun? _____

_____

_____

3. What is your favorite subject(s) in school? Why? _____

_____

_____

4. What is your least favorite subject(s) in school? Why? _____

_____

_____

5. What is your favorite food? Why? _____

_____

_____

6. What is your favorite animal? Why? _____

_____

_____

7. Where is the best or most interesting place you have ever been? Why? _____

_____

_____

8. What are some places you would like to go? Why? _____

_____

_____

9. What is something you would like to learn more about or how to do? Why? ____

_____

_____

10. What is your favorite book? Why? _____

_____

_____

11. Who is your favorite author? Why? _____

_____

_____

FIGURE 2.1. Interest survey.

1. Open to a page in the middle of the book you might select.

2. Read the page to yourself.

3. Count on your fingers any words on the page you don't know as you read.

4. If you have five or more fingers up when you are finished reading the page, the book is probably too difficult for you to read.

5. If you have no fingers up when you are finished reading the page, the book may be too easy for you too read.

6. Choose the book when you have 0–2 fingers up after you have finished reading a page.

FIGURE 2.2. Five-finger method for selecting books.

WHAT DOES A THIRD GRADER'S WRITING LOOK LIKE?

As with all areas of literacy, the writing abilities of your third graders will vary. In general, third graders must learn to sustain their writing. Whereas they may only have written one or two sentences in first grade and perhaps a paragraph by second grade, in third grade expectations for writing should increase because fluency in writing has increased (Calkins, 1986). Thus, third graders need to be encouraged to write for as long as they can and to be held to high standards for their writing products.

Our students should be able to write in a variety of ways, in a variety of situations, for a variety of purposes. For instance, third graders should be able not only to create a written piece by going through the writing process but also to write on demand. This means third graders should be able to prewrite, write a draft, confer with their peers and the teacher, edit their work, make revisions, and publish their final piece. They should be able to move through the different steps independently, although they may struggle somewhat with editing and revising. Scaffolding provided by the teacher during conferences should be geared less toward correcting mechanics and spelling and more toward content and organization. For instance, in conferences I work on paragraphing, writing appropriately for the audience, ensuring flow, and clarifying areas that might not make sense to a reader. This process is not quick—using the writing process, a student's production of a piece may take several days or even a week or two.

However, writing on demand differs in that it is usually a timed and very specific writing task. It can take the form of a response to text, a personal experience, or a response to a very specific question or set of questions. For instance, the students may be asked to read two stories and then compare the two texts in various ways.

Third graders should be able to write in paragraph form. They should be comfortable using end marks and appropriate basic sentence structure (subject/predicate). They should be gradually becoming more comfortable with commas, apostrophes, and quotation marks. Also, they should be using conventional spelling or at least be aware that a word they have written may not be spelled correctly. For instance, while editing their own writing and the writing of other students, they should be able to circle words that may not be spelled correctly. Third graders should also be increasingly aware of when to use uppercase letters. All sentences should begin with capital letters, as should proper nouns, days of the week, and months of the year. As third grade comes to an end, our students should be capitalizing holidays, titles, and so on.

Third graders should be familiar with and continuously exposed to different writing genres—letter writing, writing persuasive essays, how-to writing, writing to inform, narrative or story writing, and writing poetry. In addition, third graders should be able to respond to the texts they read in a multitude of ways, such as journal responses related to any personal or intertextual connections, summaries, or simply descriptions of their favorite part or the most important fact.

In third grade, students should be able to express themselves clearly in writing. They should be becoming increasingly aware of their audience by varying their sentences and words. Students should also be adding more details in their narrative writing, specifically with the use of more adjectives and in-depth descriptive sentences. They should also be able to reread their writing to see if what they have written makes sense and to make appropriate revisions. They should be able to use graphic organizers to aid in organizing information or ideas about a topic and rubrics to reflect on and evaluate their work.

Appropriate Goals for Writing Instruction

Goals for writing instruction in third grade could be the subject of an entire text. However, we will focus on just a few. First, provide time for teacher modeling (lots and lots of modeling). Second, give your students time to actually write. Third, provide a balance between on-demand writing tasks and those using the full writing process.

Modeling various writing genres, conventions, organization, and other important aspects of writing can take place during shared writing experiences and mini-lessons. In shared writing experiences, the teacher and students write together on chart paper, overhead, or chalkboard about a shared experience. Such writing can occur at any time—after a field trip, during the morning message, or as part of a lesson. Mini-lessons can occur during a shared writing experience, at the beginning of writing time, in small flexible groups, or during individual student conferences. Mini-lessons are 10- to 15-minute lessons designed to explicitly teach any skills related to writing. For example, as part of my initial mini-lessons for writer's workshop, I model the steps in the writing process across several days. I begin with a mini-lesson on how to determine what to write about. I think aloud about various ideas, such as my dog, surfing, making cookies, autumn, and reading. I write these ideas in my writing folder so I can refer back to them, thus always having something to write about. Then I go through each choice and brainstorm as a think-aloud what I know about each of the topics. For example, I determine that I do not know much about surfing. It's something I would like to learn more about, but right now I don't know enough to write about it. After modeling how I choose what to write about, I ask the students to start their own list of topics. A list of possible mini-lessons is found in Figure 2.3. Sigmon and Ford (2002) offer many suggestions for writing mini-lessons for third graders. However, students' progress, needs, and questions should ultimately guide the planning of your own lessons.

Another way to constantly model good writing is to use buddy journals. The teacher writes to all of the students in journals, where they record their responses

- Steps of the writing process
- On-demand writing
- Topic ideas
- Writing paragraphs (indenting)
- End marks
- What to do if you can't spell a word
- Writing complete sentences
- How to edit
- Using apostrophes
- Genres (letters, poetry, expository, persuasive)
- Setting
- Character development
- Using quotation marks
- Appropriate use of capital letters
- Adding details
- Varying sentences
- Revising
- Using pronouns
- Plot development

FIGURE 2.3. Ideas for writing mini-lessons. Based in part on Sigmon and Ford (2002).

to the books they are reading. It can be very time consuming for the teacher, but students will always have an appropriate, individual model of writing content, which can be very motivating.

As mentioned previously, the second goal is to give students ample time to write. Writing should occur across the school day for many purposes. Students can describe their findings in science, write a research report in social studies, or respond to a chapter in a book they're reading.

The third goal is to provide a balance between process writing and on-demand writing. Process writing (often accomplished during a block of time called Writers' Workshop) should occur as frequently as possible for at least one-half hour (a 5-minute mini-lesson, 20 minutes of writing, or a 5-minute share time) each day. On-demand writing assignments should be given daily. Buddy journals, writing-center tasks, and responses to literature are ways in which third-grade teachers can vary on-demand writing and allow for student choice. All of these types of writing do not have to occur at a designated time. Writing tasks can be completed by students while the teacher is working with small groups for reading, or for any subject for that matter.

Other instructional goals include helping students to become more independent writers who are increasingly more reflective about their writing and the writing of others and improving their writing conventions and organization through modeling, conferences, and guided practice. By the end of the school year, third graders should be able to write complete sentences, use paragraph form, and use correct punctuation and capitalization. They should be able to write for a specific audience, with some scaffolding, and use details and vivid words to make their writing more interesting for the reader.

SUMMARY

This chapter covered what to expect from your third graders in literacy. Students should be using a variety of ways to sound out words, and most should be in Ehri's (1991) orthographic phase, in which children analogize to known words and are able to chunk words to figure out unknown words.

Most third graders should be reading fluently, meaning that they can decode words more automatically and devote most of their time and attention to understanding what they are reading. Third graders should continue to practice reading at an appropriate rate and with expression by participating in Readers' Theater or a number of other classroom activities to strengthen and/or maintain their oral reading skills.

Third graders should also continue to build on their comprehension skills and strategies. They need to possess a variety of strategies to understand what they are reading across subject areas.

Vocabulary instruction is needed to build vocabularies and foster strategies to figure out the meanings of unknown words in a meaningful way. This instruction can also help comprehension and overall reading achievement.

Positive attitudes toward reading should be fostered, and teachers should remember that students are motivated in a variety of ways.

Finally, students should be able to write for a variety of purposes and in different situations, using appropriate conventions and organization. They should be exposed to a wide range of genres and good writing examples through modeling. Students should also be given appropriate amounts of time to write.

CHAPTER 3

SETTING UP THE ENVIRONMENT FOR LITERACY

HOW TO MOTIVATE STUDENTS FOR LITERACY

The goal of literacy instruction in any classroom is to develop lifelong readers who *can* read and who *choose* to read for a variety of purposes. By arranging our third-grade classroom environments to attend to this goal, we can reduce problems related to illiteracy and aliteracy. *Illiteracy* refers to individuals who are unable to read and write. *Aliteracy* pertains to an individual, who although able to read and write, is completely uninterested in reading and chooses to avoid it.

The most recent National Assessment of Educational Progress (NAEP) revealed that reading achievement among fourth graders has changed little in the past decade (1992–2005), with 64% reading at or above basic levels and 31% reading at or above proficient levels (Perie, Grigg, & Donahue, 2005). In international comparisons fourth graders in the United States perform significantly better than the international average in literacy, and they outperform their counterparts in 23 of the 34 countries participating in the Progress in International Reading Literacy Study 2001 (National Center for Education Statistics, 2004b). These data suggest we are doing a relatively good job of helping our students become literate through fourth grade. However, when we consider the degree to which our students are interested in reading, we have a great deal of work to do. A national survey of attitudes toward recreational and academic reading found that attitudes start out fairly positive in first grade and grow increasingly negative by sixth grade (McKenna, Kear, & Ellsworth, 1995). Third grade is a critical year for attitudes toward reading—particularly for struggling readers. McKenna et al. found that negative attitudes toward recreational reading were related to ability, with less able readers experiencing significant declines in attitude between second and third grade and fourth and fifth grade. Girls tended to have more positive attitudes toward both recreational and academic reading than boys.

In international comparisons of the reading habits of fourth graders outside of schools the Progress in International Reading Literacy Study (PIRLS) found that 35% of U.S. fourth graders reported reading for fun every day or almost every day, which was less than the international average of 40%. A nearly equivalent number (32%) of U.S. fourth graders reported never or almost never reading for fun outside of school, which was significantly higher than the international average of 18% (National Center for Education Statistics, 2004b). The PIRLS also found that in the United States and at the international level, fourth graders who read for fun every day or almost every day had higher average scores on the literacy measure than those who never or almost never read for fun. Thus, attitudes and motivation for reading play an important role not only in creating lifelong readers but also in facilitating reading achievement.

The goal of this chapter is to help you create an environment in your third-grade classroom that fosters literacy and motivation for reading. Two elements are essential to this goal: (1) creating the instructional space and (2) creating a balanced instructional program.

CREATING A SPACE THAT FOSTERS LITERACY AND MOTIVATION

What Overall Goals Do I Have for My Students and the Classroom Community?

Your classroom is a canvas. Just as the paint an artist places on canvas is an expression of his or her innermost feelings and emotions, the environment you create in your classroom is a reflection and expression of not only your instructional goals but also your pedagogical beliefs, values, and philosophy. An artist expresses via paint; however, your pedagogical beliefs, values, and philosophy are expressed through (1) the instructional materials and texts you place in your classroom, (2) the way in which you physically arrange those materials and the furniture in your room, (3) your own demeanor, and (4) the instructional program you establish for literacy (which will be examined in more detail later in the chapter).

Consider the following scenario: If a stranger were to enter your third-grade classroom, what feeling would you like him or her to have? Jot down the words or phrases that pop into your mind as you ponder this question. These ideas reflect an initial conception of the overall goals you have for your classroom environment. Thinking about and establishing these overall goals will help you plan your literate environment (see Figure 3.1).

Overall Goals	How Overall Goals Are Reflected in			
	Materials and Texts	Physical Arrangement of Materials and Furniture	Teacher Demeanor	Instructional Program
1.				
2.				
3.				
4.				

FIGURE 3.1. Planning matrix for establishing a classroom environment that fosters literacy and motivation.

From *Teaching Literacy in Third Grade* by Janice F. Almasi, Keli Garas-York, and Leigh-Ann Hildreth. Copyright 2007 by The Guilford Press. Permission to photocopy this figure is granted to purchasers of this book for personal use only (see copyright page for details).

As indicated in Figure 3.1, you should identify several overall goals—universal goals that go beyond literacy—for your classroom environment. Literacy goals might include the following: Children will read at grade level, or children will learn to use a variety of comprehension strategies while reading. In contrast, your overall goals should reflect not only your pedagogical values but also general principles that would help third graders prepare for fourth grade (beyond content goals). For example, you might believe in creating an environment that is warm and comfortable for learning, trusting, respectful of individual differences, and inclusive. Therefore, your overall goals might include creating an environment that fosters collaboration, independent learning, or learning to assume responsibility.

To illustrate, suppose you hope that strangers feel warm or comfortable when they enter your room. One of the overall goals for your literate environment would then be this: Students will feel comfortable in my classroom environment. You would plan the environment to reflect and support this goal in all four of the areas suggested above (materials and texts, physical arrangement of materials and furniture, your demeanor, and instructional program).

First, you would think about what types of instructional materials you might include in your environment to help all children in your classroom feel comfortable. You will most likely have a wide range of reading abilities and interests within a third-grade classroom. Abilities may range from very emergent reading to reading at middle school levels. Interests may range from sports to animals. Therefore, to make all children feel comfortable, you would use instructional materials and texts that reflect this range of reading abilities and interests.

Second, think about how you would organize and arrange the materials to create a comfortable environment. Comfort in the physical environment allows children to relax while reading, as well as access materials easily and on their own. You might place materials and texts in spaces where third graders can easily reach them, for example, in baskets or containers with labels denoting genre, topic, and/or reading level. Figure 3.2 depicts a third-grade classroom library in which the baskets of books are organized and labeled by topic (e.g., sports, nature, math, Magic Treehouse Books, and Babysitter's Club books) and are within reach of third-graders' hands. There are several small stools in the classroom library so children will feel comfortable. Many teachers also include beanbags, pillows, or stuffed animals to foster comfort while reading.

Third, think about your own demeanor as a teacher in this environment. How can your facial expressions, body language, speech, and actions foster comfort for your third graders? Furrowed eyebrows, crossed arms, frowns, harsh words, and negative statements send a message of dissatisfaction to your students and may create discomfort. Smiles, praise, positive statements, and scaffolded support during instruction provide a more comforting environment for fostering literacy and motivation. Often, we unconsciously communicate negative thoughts to our students through our body language. To create a comfortable learning environment, we must be consciously aware of what our facial

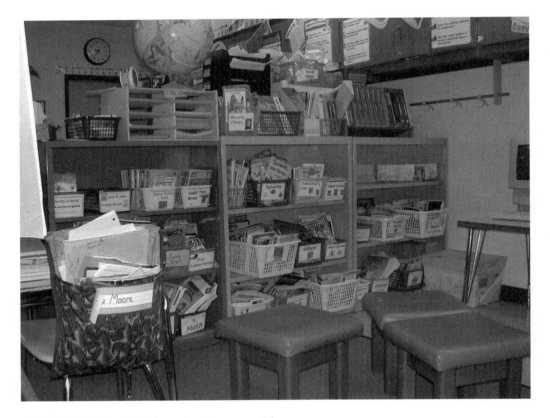

FIGURE 3.2. A third-grade classroom library.

expressions and body language can communicate and do our best not to transfer unintended messages to our students.

Finally, consider how you might help students feel comfortable in your instructional program, that is, by providing literacy instruction that is developmentally appropriate for each student's individual needs and materials that are at each student's instructional level. Difficult texts and materials lead to frustration and negative attitudes toward reading. Texts that are too easy do not provide enough challenge to enhance children's reading abilities and sustain their motivation. Therefore, to attain a comfortable learning environment, texts used for literacy instruction need to be at just the right level.

The example above shows how one might structure the physical environment, the materials, one's own demeanor, and the instructional program. However, you must also establish your own overall goals for your third graders.

The goals teachers set for their classroom are reflected in multiple ways, and incongruity between any two aspects of the literate environment will send mixed messages to your students. If your goal is to create a comfortable learning environment, reflected by the materials and texts, but the physical arrangement of the furniture, your own demeanor, or some aspect of your instructional program conflicts with your goal, the students will become confused. Such incongruity sends conflicting signals to the children, creating discord and discontinuity in your literate environment. Thus, prior planning and thoughtful coordination are essential in creating a harmonic and cohesive atmosphere in your classroom.

The Physical Environment: What Should My Classroom Look Like to Attain These Goals?

Having considered the goals you would like to see reflected in your classroom, we now consider the physical environment in more detail. As noted earlier, third grade is a critical period with regard to motivation for reading. The physical environment of your classroom can significantly help to sustain, maintain, and enhance students' motivation. Research has shown that making a variety of literacy materials handy to the students is critical to their literacy development (Neuman, 1999). The physical arrangement of materials and furniture work in conjunction with one another to create and sustain an environment that fosters literacy. Wherever possible, your classroom should exude literacy. That is, a wide variety of materials for reading and writing should be abundant and attainable throughout the room.

First, consider the physical arrangement of furniture. The way in which students' desks are configured provides hints about a teacher's pedagogical beliefs, values, and philosophy. Examine the way in which students' desks are configured in Figures 3.3 and 3.4. What does the direction in which students are facing suggest about the teacher's pedagogical philosophy? Arrangements such as those in Figure 3.3, in which students are facing the teacher's desk and the white board, indicate a teacher-centered classroom in which the teacher instructs via lectures and students have little opportunity to collaborate, although students may on occasion have the opportunity for paired activities. The presence of learning centers and tables in Figure 3.4, however, suggests a different pedagogical philosophy, one in which instruction is student-centered and highly collaborative.

Figure 3.3 shows only one space, at the back of the room, where children have access to books. The students' backs are turned to the only visible literacy material in the room, and those students at the front would have to wind through the desks of other children to reach the books. Thus, the physical environment suggests that this teacher is not overtly creating a space dedicated to fostering interest in and motivation for literacy.

In contrast, Figure 3.4 shows many points of access to literacy materials and texts. Four sets of bookshelves are scattered around the room, and the literacy center is in a prominent place in the center. The two bookshelves, rug, and beanbags provide a comfortable and enticing spot to motivate students to select and enjoy texts. The writing center is also positioned in the center of the room, giving all students easy access to writing materials, computers, and additional books. The science/math, social studies, and art centers provide further opportu-

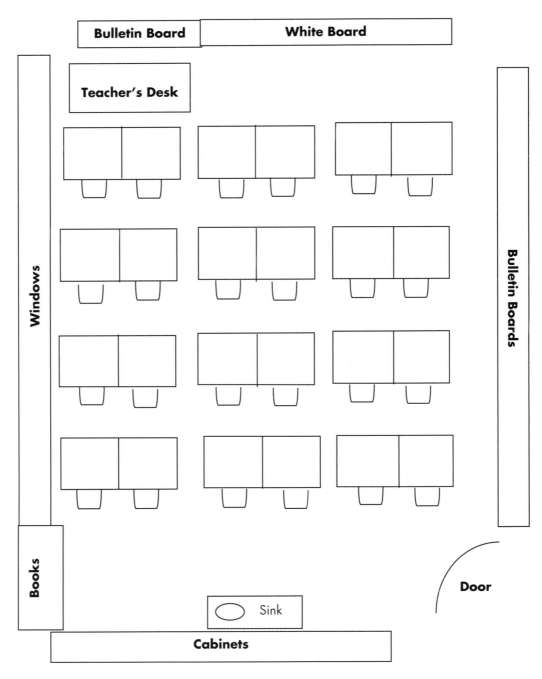

FIGURE 3.3. Classroom physical arrangement 1.

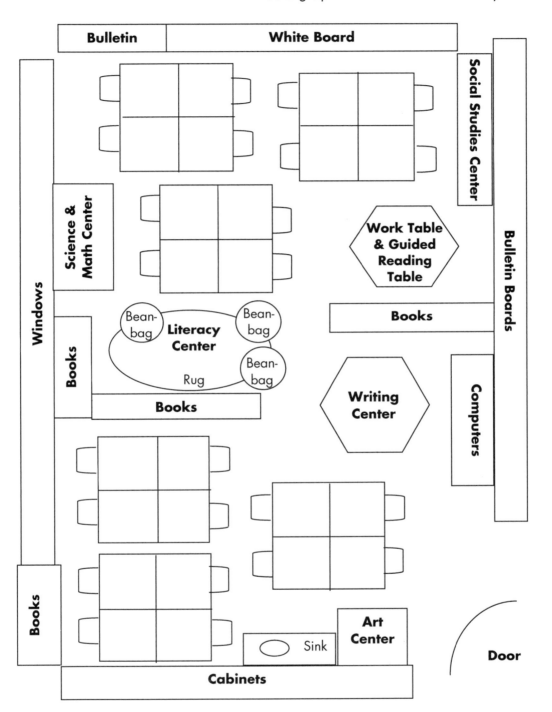

FIGURE 3.4. Classroom physical arrangement 2.

nity for literacy engagement through explorations of informational text and collab-orative projects and activities focused on content. Thus, no student in the room is far from some form of literacy material. The presence of learning centers suggests that this teacher values free choice and individualized instruction, as well as student responsibility and independence.

How Should I Arrange the Physical Environment to Promote Literacy?

When planning your physical environment, it is critical to first establish your over-all goals (e.g., comfort, respect, and responsibility) for your students and then con-sider how the environment might be arranged to attain them. It is also critical to consider how the physical environment might be arranged to promote goals spe-cific to literacy and motivation for literacy.

Fountas and Pinnell (1996, p. 44) have suggested that "literacy-rich" environ-ments include seven areas in the classroom: (1) a large-group area, (2) small-group areas, (3) independent work areas, (4) a guided reading area, (5) a print-rich class-room, (6) a classroom library, and (7) centers.

Large-Group Area

The large-group area allows the teacher to meet with the entire class. In this space teachers might teach a mini-lesson, do a read-aloud, or have a class meeting. The intent is to create a cozy meeting space. Many teachers use a large rug as the desig-nated large-group area, and others use the classroom library. In Figure 3.3, the teacher could create a large-group meeting area at the front or back of the room. In Figure 3.4, the teacher could use the rug area, where the beanbags are located, for the large-group meeting.

Small-Group Areas

Small-group areas can be used for groups of two to five students. The purpose of a small-group area is to provide space where students can read, write, think, talk, and create together. That is, the children can co-construct their interpretations of text and learn to work with one another. Each small-group area can be created by separating tables or groups of desks from other areas of the room with low book shelves or dividers. These areas should have a sufficient number of chairs and an ample supply of materials so that children can work on projects related to texts they are reading or work in learning centers. Figure 3.3 does not designate any space for small-group work, but Figure 3.4 shows multiple spaces (e.g., the writ-ing, art, science/math, and social studies centers). The students' desks are also arranged in clusters, which makes it easy for students to temporarily transform each cluster into a small-group work area.

Independent Work Areas

Children should also have space to work independently, for example, the desks in both Figures 3.3 and 3.4. However, Figure 3.4 also shows independent space at the computer area. In independent work areas, students also need personal space to store their work and their supplies. If desks have an open space for storing materials, this will suffice. Some classrooms use "chair packs" (visible on the back of the chair in Figure 3.2), where independent work is easily accessible.

Teacher-Guided Reading Instruction Area

The guided reading area allows the teacher to give literacy instruction to small groups of children. This space should be in a quiet section of the room. However, you want to be sure you have a clear view of all students, particularly those not at the guided reading area. While you are instructing one small group of students, the rest of the class will be either working on independent literacy projects, on small-group projects, or in learning centers. Therefore, you need to be able to see all other students in case they may need assistance. Figure 3.4 shows a separate guided reading area on the right side of the classroom. Given that instruction will occur in this space, you might consider adding an easel with chart paper or a pocket chart to model literacy strategies during instruction. You will also need easy access to writing materials such as markers, pencils, sentence strips, and paper.

Print-Rich Classroom

Fountas and Pinnell (1996, p. 44) suggest that the physical environment be filled with a wide variety of printed work. They recommend, however, that the environment should not become littered with what they call "static materials" such as helper charts and birthday charts. Instead, they recommend a large range of children's literature, charts of poems and songs, labels and directions for materials at learning centers, informational texts, word walls, child-authored writing, message boards, mailboxes, and other print materials that will foster authentic uses for reading and writing. These materials should be at eye level and easily accessible.

Classroom Library

Your third-grade classroom should include a small library, or "book nook," which features a variety of reading materials that span a wide range of reading abilities. Many teachers organize the texts in their classroom library in small bins or baskets (as in Figure 3.2) by genre. This enables children to easily locate texts of interest. It also assists in teaching children how to sort and classify texts when they are searching for and reshelving them.

The classroom library should be inviting. As depicted in the diagram in Figure 3.4, many teachers include beanbags, cushions, or pillows to invite children to relax while they read. Many teachers also create their classroom libraries around themes to motivate children. For example, if you were planning an integrated unit around an adventure or camping theme, you might add a small tent to your classroom as a special place where one or two children could go to read (see Figure 3.5). If you were studying oceans and decorated your classroom with theme-related stimuli such as fish and other aquatic creatures, you might add a "shark cage" made of chicken wire and boards to your classroom library to create a safe place for children to read for fun. Although these special reading nooks take a bit of time and effort to prepare, as well as some space in your classroom, the added benefit of having a motivating place where children are excited to read is well worth the effort.

Learning Centers

Learning centers are also important in third-grade classrooms because they provide opportunities for students to have a choice in the types of activities in which they engage. Fountas and Pinnell (1996, p. 49) define a center as "a physical area set aside for specific learning purposes." Centers contain the requisite materials to enable students to discover, create, and work independently, with a partner, or with a small group. The tasks in learning centers should enable students to be active learners and should promote open-ended inquiry (Fountas & Pinnell, 1996).

FIGURE 3.5. A comfortable space for children to read.

When we provide open-ended tasks that are challenging and allow for choice, students become more motivated to engage in literacy-related activities (Turner, 1995). Unfortunately, many of the tasks we give students are closed-ended, such as practice activities and worksheets (e.g., drill and skill work, matching exercises, fill-in-the-blank activities, and multiple-choice questions). The information used to complete closed-ended tasks is often provided by the teacher and is expected to be used in a similar manner by all the students to produce expected (and identical) solutions. These activities do not offer students the opportunity to make decisions because the task, the way it should be completed, and its outcome are determined in advance. Turner's research found that such tasks lead to decreased motivation for literacy for young children.

Open-ended tasks, on the other hand, are those in which students "frame the problem and design a solution" (Turner, 1995, p. 424), which require students to identify relevant information and decide how to use it to solve a problem. In other words, open-ended tasks require students to engage in critical thinking, in which they question, analyze, make inferences, evaluate, and judge (see Figure 3.6). Open-ended tasks also require students to be metacognitive and to make decisions.

Critical thinking involves:

- A questioning attitude
- Logical analysis
- Inference
- Evaluation
- Judgment

Open-ended tasks

- Require inference, evaluation, judgment
- Have multiple possibilities for answers

Closed-ended tasks

- Have predetermined or known answers
- Have right/wrong answers

FIGURE 3.6. Keys to critical thinking and analysis.

Literacy centers provide a golden opportunity to engage students in open-ended tasks. Third-grade classrooms might contain some permanent centers such as the literacy center/library, the writing center, and the art center (see Figure 3.4). In the literacy center, students select books for independent or partner reading. Thus, the task is open-ended in that students must make decisions about the texts they want to read and how they go about reading them (strategy use). Similarly, in the writing center, students select the type of writing in which they want to engage. The composing process requires students to engage in decision-making and problem-solving behaviors as they pertain to brainstorming, composing, revising, and editing. The art center also gives children the opportunity to select materials and engage in the creative process of visually representing their ideas. In terms of literacy, the art center might be a place where students create visual responses to the literature they read, props for dramatizing literature, or materials for use in presentations.

Science, math, and social studies centers may be permanent, but the topics for exploration may change according to the content being covered in class. For example, if your third-grade curriculum includes the study of life cycles, the science center might give students the opportunity to engage in an open-ended and ongoing inquiry project in which they document the growth of a plant or the life cycle of a butterfly. Texts related to the unit, journals, rulers, graph paper, and colored pencils could be placed in the science center to facilitate the inquiry. Children could go to the center to check the growth or development of the plant or butterfly, measure and record its growth, describe what they observe in their journal, draw a picture of it, and note new questions or hypotheses. In this manner, not only scientific inquiry is promoted but also reading, writing, and critical thinking.

If the third-grade social studies curriculum is focused on communities, the social studies learning center might give students the chance to design and conduct interviews with various members of the local community. They could decide what questions they might ask various community members, design their interviews, and after conducting interviews (either face to face, by telephone, or by e-mail), work in the center to create ways in which to synthesize and communicate their findings.

These examples show how centers can be used to foster literacy and motivation for literacy by providing students with open-ended tasks that permit them to have choices and challenge them to use higher level and critical thinking skills to decide how to gather information and formulate solutions.

Summary

The physical environment is an essential part of the literacy program and should be given careful thought and planning. As in any other grade, third-grade teachers must approach such planning with careful deliberation. It begins with thinking about and establishing goals for your classroom. From there you should plan every aspect of your physical environment to support and reflect your goals.

HOW TO CREATE A BALANCED INSTRUCTIONAL PROGRAM FOSTERING LITERACY AND MOTIVATION

The students in your third-grade classroom are individuals and reflect varying degrees of development in their ability to identify and recognize words, read fluently, comprehend text, interpret text, access their background knowledge, and approach text strategically. Likewise their interests and motivations vary. Your instruction should aim to meet children where they are developmentally. Thus, your instructional program must reflect balance so you can provide each child with what he or she needs to grow as a reader, writer, and thinker. According to Morrow (2002), literacy programs should include balance in strategies, structures, and materials. They should consist of opportunities for (1) teacher read-alouds, (2) shared reading, (3) teacher-guided reading instruction, and (4) independent reading. Morrow has also highlighted the importance of (5) reading and writing collaboratively with peers, (6) sharing completed reading and writing activities, and (7) making content connections for reading and writing. This section will focus on the first four elements and explain how you might integrate collaborative reading and writing, performance, and content. Tompkins and McGee (1993) recommend using each program element according to your instructional purpose, the availability of reading materials, and students' proficiency. They also explain that all four elements may occur in some classrooms daily, whereas in other classrooms, teachers and students may use only two or three elements daily. At least two of these program elements should occur daily, and over the course of the year all four should be used.

Teacher Read-Alouds

The teacher read-aloud is one of the most important programmatic elements in your literacy program. Read-alouds occur when the teacher reads text aloud to students. When the term *read-aloud* is used in this text, we are referring to *teacher* read-alouds. This term should not be confused with the practice of having *students* read text aloud, a form of which is also known as "round robin reading." We frown upon this practice, which will be discussed in more detail in the shared reading section.

Why Are Teacher Read-Alouds Important?

Read-alouds serve several purposes in a literacy program: (1) models of good, fluent oral reading; (2) cognitive benefits; and (3) affective benefits.

COGNITIVE BENEFITS

Read-alouds provide a host of positive cognitive benefits for your third graders. When children have the opportunity to hear stories read aloud, they hear how fluent oral reading should sound. This helps them understand how their own reading should "sound" inside their minds as they read silently to themselves. Research has also shown that vocabulary and comprehension are enhanced through read-alouds (Krashen, 2004). When students hear unfamiliar words in the context of a story or text, the new word becomes part of their listening (or receptive) vocabulary. That is, the word becomes one they have heard and can at least recognize when others use it to communicate. After students hear the word a few more times in context, it may become part of their spoken (or expressive) vocabulary. By listening to stories read aloud, students also indirectly learn how texts are structured, as well as learning about the author's style, author's craft, and the story's genre. Through such exposure, students gradually internalize these important stylistic elements of text. Thus, read-alouds give students three cognitive benefits: (1) fluency, (2) vocabulary and comprehension, and (3) an understanding of style.

AFFECTIVE BENEFITS

Read-alouds also provide affective, or motivational, benefits, what Krashen (2004, p. 78) calls an "indirect effect" on literacy development. That is, when students simply engage in the process of hearing and discussing stories, further reading is encouraged. Most children enjoy read-alouds because they are fun. If they are done well, read-alouds provide the opportunity to create interest and motivation for reading, which creates a positive attitude toward reading. Daily read-alouds also provide an opportunity to model literate behaviors as part of everyday life.

Planning Teacher Read-Alouds

Teacher read-alouds should not become a "filler" event when there are spare minutes in the instructional day or after recess. They should be an integral part of the planned instructional program.

SELECT TEXTS PURPOSEFULLY

Select texts for read-alouds that suit your students' interests, reflect content, or allow you to model reading strategies you have taught. Because you are reading the books to your third graders, these texts can (and should) have a higher readability than those students can read on their own. You might consider selecting texts above your students' instructional reading levels. In this way, you are exposing them to vocabulary, language structures, and text structure that may be too difficult for them to read on their own. This enhances and contributes to their growth as readers.

SELECT A VARIETY OF TEXTS FOR INCLUSION IN YOUR READ-ALOUD PROGRAM

Generally, most third graders enjoy read-alouds of any type of text. Therefore, your read-aloud program is a tremendous opportunity to introduce your students to a variety of genres and styles. Although third graders love hilarious picture books and poems, it is important to expose them to the beauty of all text types and content, including serious subject matter in both narrative and informational texts. They should include (1) wordless books, (2) predictable books, (3) picture books, (4) novels, (5) poetry, (6) informational texts, and (7) award-winning texts.

Wordless books are often used with emergent readers to engage them in the reading process. They are also wonderful for teaching emergent readers about print conventions, such as left-to-right progression. However, wordless picture books can also be used in third-grade classrooms as a stimulus for writing. Some wordless texts you could present to the class are Raymond Briggs's (1978) *The Snowman*, Tomie dePaola's (1978) *Pancakes for Breakfast*, Pat Hutchins's (1968) *Rosie's Walk*, or Emily Arnold McCully's (1985) *First Snow*. Following the read-aloud, you could model how students could use the pictures as a stimulus for writing their own version of the wordless picture book. After modeling, you could place the book in your writing center and offer students the opportunity to create their own written versions of the text to accompany the pictures.

Predictable books are enjoyable to use as read-alouds because they allow students to join in. Although they may seem more appropriate for younger children, they can be used with third graders to model fluent oral reading and promote participation when predictable portions are read. Books are considered predictable if some aspect of the text is repeated. The repeated portion could be a *phrase*, as in Judith Viorst's (1972) classic *Alexander and the Terrible, Horrible, No Good, Very Bad Day*, in which the phrase "terrible, horrible, no good, very bad day" is repeated throughout the narrative. A text may also be considered predictable if it has a *predictable plot*. Classic tales such as Paul Galdone's (1970) *The Three Little Pigs* or K. Y. Craft's (2000) *Cinderella* have a predictable plot to use as a cornerstone in teaching students about plot structure or how to make text-to-text connections (intertextual connections). The predictable Cinderella plot could be introduced in a read-aloud of Craft's *Cinderella*. Afterward, small groups of students could select another version of the same tale (see Figure 3.7) to read for guided reading instruction. Each small group might then compare and contrast the version read aloud with the version they read for guided reading, or they might also compare their versions with versions read by other small groups.

Predictable texts may also have a *cumulative pattern* or plot. For example, Linda Williams's (1986) *The Little Old Lady Who Was Not Afraid of Anything* involves a little old lady who takes a walk in the woods one night. As she is walking, she encounters two big shoes, which go CLOMP, CLOMP, giving her a temporary fright, but she bravely says, "Go away you two big shoes I'm not afraid of you." Later she encounters a pair of pants that go WIGGLE WIGGLE, a shirt that goes SHAKE SHAKE, two gloves, a hat, and a pumpkin head, which also try to frighten her. As she encounters each new object, all of the previous objects and their frightening sounds are repeated in the order in which the old lady met them. Such cumulative patterns encourage students to join in during the read-aloud, which develops fluency.

Climo, S. (1989). *The Egyptian Cinderella*. New York: HarperCollins.
Climo, S. (1996). *The Irish Cinderlad*. New York: HarperCollins.
Climo, S. (1993). *The Korean Cinderella*. New York: HarperTrophy.
Climo, S. (1999). *The Persian Cinderella*. New York: HarperCollins.
Craft, K. Y. (2000). *Cinderella*. New York: SeaStar Books.
Hickox, R. (1998). *The golden sandal: A Middle Eastern Cinderella story*. New York: Holiday House.
Louie, A. (1987). *Yeh-Shen: A Cinderella story from China*. New York: Puffin Books.
Martin, R. (1992). *The rough/ace girl*. New York: Penguin Putnam Books. (An Algonquin Cinderella story)
Perrault, C. (1999). *Cinderella*. New York: North-South Books.
Pollock, P. (1996). *The turkey girl: A Zuni Cinderella story*. New York: Little, Brown.
San Souci, R. D. (1998). *Cendrillon: A Caribbean Cinderella*. New York: Simon & Schuster.
Schroeder, A. (1997). *Smoky Mountain Rose: An Appalachian Cinderella*. New York: Puffin Books.

FIGURE 3.7. Versions and variants of the Cinderella story.

Picture books that tell a story are often read aloud. In Chapters 5 and 7, Leigh-Ann Hildreth lists a number of picture books her third graders enjoy, which will provide a start to your read-aloud collection.

In the past decade, publishing companies have done a remarkable job of publishing vivid nonfiction picture books. Their color photographs, illustrations, and diagrams entice third-grade readers into the world of informational text. Authors and publishers have learned to include features attractive to young readers. That is, these texts do not offer pages and pages of lengthy descriptions and explanations of content, as in the past. Instead they have brief chunks of text surrounded by photographs, illustrations, diagrams, and charts to explain the content in a more eye-catching, reader-friendly manner. Examples of some informational texts appealing to third graders include the *Science of Living Things Series*, written by Bobbie Kalman and published by Crabtree. These stunning texts use photographs, charts, illustrations, and a brief text to explain such scientific concepts as *What Is a Life Cycle?* (1998), *What Is a Biome?* (1998), *What Is a Plant?* (2000), *What Are Camouflage and Mimicry?* (2001), and *What Are Food Chains and Webs?* (1998). Third graders also enjoy Gail Gibbons's books, which are developmentally appropriate and use clear drawings to depict such scientific concepts as *The Reasons for Seasons* (1995), *From Seed to Plant* (1991), *Deserts* (1996), *Spiders* (1993), and *Recycle! A Handbook for Kids* (1992). Steve Jenkins's *Actual Size* (2004) uses beautiful torn-paper collages to depict 18 different animals or parts of animals in their actual size. Texts such as *Flash, Crash, Rumble, and Roll* by Franklyn Branley (1985) provide interesting explanations of weather-related events such as thunder and lightning, and K. Zoehfeld's (1995) *How Mountains Are Made* (1995) uses illustrations, diagrams, and cause–effect text structure to explain theories of plate tectonics in language appropriate for third graders. Books like these stimulate interest in content and help young readers internalize the structures of informational text.

Short novels and longer novels (chapter books) enable students to hear stories with longer and more complex plots. Short novels such as Sharon Creech's *Love That Dog* (2001), Roald Dahl's *Fantastic Mr. Fox* (1988), Sid Fleischman's *The Whipping Boy* (1986), John Reynolds Gardner's *Stone Fox* (1980), Mildred D. Taylor's *Mississippi Bridge* (1990), and Doris B. Smith's *A Taste of Blackberries* (1973) are well-written, with compelling plots that pique third graders' interests. Longer novels provide similar benefits. Patrick Skene Catling's *The Chocolate Touch* (1952), Beverly Cleary's *Dear Mr. Henshaw* (1983), Kate DiCamillo's *Because of Winn Dixie* (2000), Elizabeth George Speare's *The Sign of the Beaver* (1983), and Louis Sachar's *Holes* (1998) can be read aloud in their entirety, or several chapters could serve as an introduction to the book and a means of enticing students to either read the rest of it on their own or complete the novel during small-group guided reading lessons.

Poetry is an essential genre in a read-aloud program. The meter, rhythm, and patterned regularity display the beauty of written language to your students. Shel Silverstein's *Where the Sidewalk Ends* (1974), Kalli Dakos's *If You're Not Here, Please Raise Your Hand: Poems about School* (1990), and Wade Hudson's edited collection of poems entitled *Pass It On: African-American Poetry for Children* (1993) are classic collections.

Although your read-aloud program should include all types of texts, award-winning books are important because they have undergone scrutiny and have been honored for exceptional writing, illustration, or contributions to cultural awareness: (1) The John Newbery Medal is awarded for the most distinguished contribution to American literature for children; (2) the Randolph Caldecott Medal honors the artist of the most distinguished American picture book for children; (3) the Coretta Scott King Award honors African American authors and illustrators for outstanding contributions to children's literature promoting a better understanding and appreciation of the American dream; (4) the Laura Ingalls Wilder Award is given to an author or illustrator whose books have made a substantial and lasting contribution to children's literature; (5) the Mildred D. Batchelder Award is given to an American publisher for a work considered to be the most outstanding children's book, originally published in a foreign language in a foreign country, that has been translated into English and published in the United States; (6) the Pura Belpré Award honors a Latino/Latina writer and illustrator whose work best portrays, affirms, and celebrates the Latino cultural experience in an outstanding work of children's literature; (7) the Robert F. Sibert Informational Book Medal is awarded to the author of the most distinguished informational book; and (8) the Theodor Seuss Geisel Award honors the author and illustrator of the most distinguished contribution to the body of American children's literature known as beginning reader books.

ORGANIZE YOUR READ-ALOUDS

As you plan your read-aloud program, be sure to arrange a predictable time for this event daily. Preview and preread the texts you plan to use before reading them aloud to students. Some texts may be excellent for silent reading but do not lend themselves to read-alouds. Likewise, you should be familiar with the text in advance so your own reading is fluent. If your students are young or not used to a daily read-aloud program, you may want to begin by reading aloud for just a few minutes each day. As students become accustomed to the read-aloud, gradually increase the number of minutes in hopes of building up to 20–30 minutes each day.

TIPS FOR READING ALOUD

Wolf (2004, p. 99) suggests that teachers read aloud with "panache." That is, your reading should be filled with enthusiasm and expression. Your read-aloud should help students with interpretation by providing intonation, accent, and vocal characterization where appropriate. Your students should be moved by the text so that they become excited by it and learn to appreciate its value and beauty.

Types of Teacher Read-Alouds

Your read-aloud program provides an opportunity to help students learn to read for a variety of purposes. Therefore, the read-aloud portion of your literacy block should include reading (1) for pleasure, (2) to inform, (3) to communicate a message, (4) to expose your students to new genres, and (5) to model reading strategies.

READ FOR PLEASURE

One of the most frequent (and important) functions of a read-aloud is to introduce students to the pleasures of reading. Texts selected for this purpose should be enjoyable, and the read-aloud should be low-key and comfortable. The read-aloud might occur in the literacy center or on a rug, where students can lie on pillows or beanbags and relax. Your demeanor should be relaxed rather than rushed, hurried, or harried. You will know if you have been successful when students are disappointed to learn the read-aloud has ended. If you hear a chorus of disgruntled "awww's" or "Please read more!" as you finish the read-aloud for the day, you will know you have attained your objective.

READ TO INFORM

Read-alouds can also be used to model how students can locate texts and read them to gain new information. Very often students come up with excellent and perplexing questions about the subjects being studied. Use your read-aloud to model locating texts (e.g., informational texts or online resources) and then read aloud relevant portions to acquire insights into the question. Reading aloud for this purpose will help students' critical thinking, and students will learn that true learning is a never-ending process of inquiry and discovery.

READ TO COMMUNICATE A MESSAGE

Your third-grade classroom is a community of learners who work and reside together for 6–7 hours each day, 5 days per week, for one-half of a year. Problems and difficult situations are inherent to any community or culture. In a third-grade classroom, social problems such as tattling, name calling, taunting, and bullying of all types (physical, verbal, and relational) often occur, making some students feel lonely and isolated from their classmates. Victims of bullying can develop low self-esteem, depression, isolation, fear, helplessness, poor academic achievement, and high rates of absenteeism (as cited in Anti-Defamation League, 2005). Bibliotherapy, or using books to heal, is a way to address the social and personal problems that occur throughout the year.

The Anti-Defamation League (ADL) sponsors a website "ADL Curriculum Connections" (www.adl.org/education/curriculum_connections) which provides antibias lesson plans and resources for K–12 educators. The Winter 2005 issue of the ADL's Curriculum Connections focuses on using children's literature to increase empathy and help students cope with bullying. This website offers research-based information on bullying (and a multitude of other topics), statistics and studies on bullying, an annotated bibliography of children's literature on bullying, how to use children's literature to overcome bullying, discussion guides, and extension activities. When selecting children's literature for bibliotherapy, the ADL website recommends selecting realistic stories that are developmentally appropriate and relevant to students' lives. Texts with these characteristics give emotional support to children by letting them know they are not alone in their feelings.

The benefit of bibliotherapy is that it enables students to talk about characters rather than themselves, which may help them discuss sensitive issues openly. Of course, your school counselor and/or school psychologist should be alerted immediately so they can assist with such problems. However, along with these highly qualified professionals, you can and should also be instrumental in helping your students generate constructive resolutions.

Some recent developmentally appropriate texts for third graders related to bullying include *My Secret Bully* (2003) by Trudy Ludwig; *Nobody Knew What to Do* (2001) by Becky Ray McCain; *Nothing Wrong with a Three-Legged Dog* (2000) by Graham McNamee; *Wings* (2000) by Christopher Myers; and *Say Something* (2004) by Margaret Paula Moss. Other classic texts related to bullying are Eleanor Estes's *The Hundred Dresses* (1974), Tomie DePaola's *Oliver Button Is a Sissy* (1979), and Nicholasa Mohr's *Felita* (1979). Carl Bosch's *Bully on the Bus* (1988) is written in a format in which readers decide what actions to take in dealing with a bully (ignoring the bully, talking to an adult, confronting the bully, fighting, and reconciling) by choosing their own ending.

Your students may also experience personal problems such as a death in the family, the death of a pet, and the need to wear glasses or braces. Like social problems, personal problems can be addressed through bibliotherapy during the read-aloud. The first step is to locate a credible and professional source to assist you in locating texts and resources. Your school counselor or school psychologist should be able to help you understand the research base for the problem, and your school library/media specialist and reading specialist may be able to help you locate credible texts, materials, and resources.

READ-ALOUD TO EXPOSE STUDENTS TO NEW GENRES

Traditionally, genre has been a means of classifying types of literature. However, Wolf (2004, p. 51) has noted that the boundaries of varied genres are often "porous," with particular stories often moving between different categories and occurring within multiple categories. Genre is seen today as more of a way for readers to understand and transform their worlds and as a way of accomplishing particular purposes through social action. The read-aloud, as noted earlier, provides a wonderful opportunity to introduce your students to a variety of text types and new genres.

In her descriptions of genres, Wolf (2004, p. 53) offers two general categories of narrative text: reality and fantasy. She describes the reality genre as stories "that could happen in the real world, marked by plausible issues and authentic problems," and she identifies subgenres, which include problem realism, historical fiction, mysteries, and animal stories. The fantasy genre is characterized as stories "of an alternative world, marked by broad flights of the imagination, talking animals, and magical forces" (p. 53). Subgenres include folk/fairy tales, fables, tall tales/legends, high fantasy, myths, and science fiction.

Informational texts should be included as yet another genre. These texts are arranged in five different patterns: (1) description (attribute, explanation, and definition/example), (2) collection (sequence, enumeration, and time order), (3) comparison (similarity/difference), (4) antecedent/consequence (cause/effect relationships), and (5) response rhetorical (problem/solution, question/answer, and remark/reply) (Meyer, 1975). An entire informational text may not be organized in one pattern. Sometimes several different patterns exist within the same chapter. This is what makes reading informational texts difficult for young readers. Thus, it is critical to begin exposing your students to a variety of patterns. The read-aloud is a perfect place to gently introduce them to your third graders.

READ-ALOUD TO MODEL HOW TO USE READING STRATEGIES

Not only can your read-aloud program provide an opportunity for you to model fluent oral reading, motivate students, and help them learn to read for a variety of purposes, it can also serve as a tool for your guided reading lessons. That is, during your read-alouds you can model the types of cognitive thoughts and strategies you use while you are reading, such as visualizing the text, making connections to prior knowledge, making predictions, questioning, and monitoring your understanding. This can be accomplished by stopping at various points and verbalizing the cognitive processes or thoughts that occur to you while you read. This procedure is called a "think-aloud." You can approach the entire read-aloud, or just portions of it, as a think-aloud. The purpose is to model the internal cognitive processes and thoughts good readers engage in while reading. Before reading you might point out the title, think aloud about its meaning in relation to the images on the front cover, and generate some predictions or set purposes for reading. While reading you might engage in think-alouds in which you update and revise your predictions as warranted by the text. You might ask questions, wonder why characters behave as they do in the text, speculate about how the problem in the story will be resolved, or describe the mental images you "see" as you read portions of the text that are extremely image-laden. Any strategy you might teach your students during guided reading can be modeled during your read-alouds. In fact, the read-aloud is a perfect place for introducing students to strategy use, whether comprehension or word identification.

How Do I Fit Teacher Read-Alouds into My Schedule?

Although you should have a regularly scheduled time each day for your read-aloud, it does not need to fit neatly into your literacy block. Read-alouds can occur during math, science, and social studies. They fit especially well at the beginning of a new unit of study to introduce your students to the topic or theme. The read-aloud should not, however, become a rationale for reading the content textbook to your class. Each content area requires a hands-on curriculum rather than a "read the textbook and answer the questions" curriculum. The read-aloud should enhance and supplement content curriculum.

Shared Reading

Shared reading is another vital component of a balanced literacy program. In shared reading students can see and follow along with the text being read, usually in unison with at least one other individual. In shared reading children are not expected to read aloud alone and they are not expected to read aloud without having practiced until they are fluent. Instructional activities such as buddy/partner/paired reading, choral reading, Readers' Theater, the Language Experience Approach, and the Shared Book Experience are all examples of shared reading.

Shared reading does *not*, however, include round robin reading, in which students are called on to read orally one after the other. Sometimes students are called on to read any amount of text (e.g., sentences, paragraphs, or pages) in any order. That is, teachers may call on random students to read one after the other, the teacher may have students go around the room in order one after the other, or students may call on other students to read. The practice is common in elementary classrooms.

Although many teachers might mistakenly believe that round robin reading facilitates oral reading and fluency, research does not support this belief. In fact, round robin reading is inferior to shared reading in every possible way. It not only leads to lower scores on every measure of reading achievement but it also leads to higher levels of anxiety and embarrassment for students. This method actually gives students very little time to practice reading because they do not read for very long and they do not practice reading or rereading (National Reading Panel, 2000). In a study comparing the effects of shared reading and round robin reading on students' reading ability, Eldridge, Reutzel, and Hollingsworth (1996) found that students who participated in shared reading had significantly higher scores on word analysis, comprehension, and vocabulary measures than their peers who participated in round robin reading. Likewise, students participating in shared reading had significantly fewer oral reading errors and higher fluency rates than their peers in round robin reading. In short, there is no good empirically validated reason to engage in round robin reading in any form—it does not promote better reading achievement on any measure, and it can lead to emotional problems.

Despite its dismal track record, some teachers insist that round robin reading is needed. They believe it is justified if they select only stronger readers to read orally. Unfortunately, this practice only serves to reinforce feelings of superiority and inferiority among students. Many teachers claim that students enjoy round robin reading and that those who struggle the most are often the first to volunteer. To this we answer that young children often do not know what is best for them. Many young children would also elect to eat candy and sweets for dinner and wear shorts on cold days. However, it is up to a knowledgeable and caring adult to plan instruction to benefit all children in the class. These children do not realize that other children will hear their disfluency during oral reading. They may not realize that some ill-mannered students may make fun of them, which could lead to low self-esteem and anxiety. As teachers, we know this may happen, and it is up to us to design a safe environment that promotes literacy and motivation.

As if the above were not enough to eradicate round robin reading, some teachers believe that it is the only way they can "hear" how students read. Opitz and Rasinski (1998) offer 25 effective alternatives to round robin reading, which they believe has the potential to cause several problems: giving students an inaccurate view of reading, causing faulty reading habits, causing unnecessary subvocalization (vocalizing words while reading silently), causing inattentive behaviors, causing anxiety and embarrassment, hampering listening comprehension, and consuming valuable class time because of the slower rate at which oral rather than silent reading proceeds. Round robin reading is an ineffective and potentially harmful instructional practice that has no place in elementary classrooms. As an alternative, we strongly recommend shared reading/writing activities.

Why Is Shared Reading Important?

As noted in Chapter 2, upon entering third grade most readers have moved beyond emergent phases of reading development and are beginning to become fluent readers. Therefore, third grade is the prime time in which to continue developing and enhancing fluency. Fluent reading requires speed, accuracy, and proper expression (National Reading Panel, 2000). Reading expressively involves reading with few and short pauses, reading with intonation, using the rise and fall of pitch, and using stress or loudness to communicate the intended message. Thus, fluency is important not only for developing children's ability to recognize words quickly and accurately but also for enhancing comprehension (Schwanenflugel, Hamilton, Kuhn, Wisenbaker, & Stahl, 2004).

How Does Shared Reading Look in Third Grade?

To develop speed, accuracy, and expression, shared reading activities must involve authentic, or connected, text, rather than practicing and rereading words in isolation.

HOW DO I PLAN AND IMPLEMENT SHARED READING?

First, select texts that are fun to read orally. You might choose those with patterned, predictable language (e.g., rhyming, repetitious vocabulary, repetitious phrases, or familiar plots), perhaps including poems, rhymes, or song lyrics. The repetition helps children by reducing the number of new words to decode or recognize, and the rhythm helps them use the prosodic features of the text (pitch, stress, tone, and pauses) so they can be more expressive.

Second, plan instructional lessons in which children learn how to recognize features of fluent oral reading and to practice their own oral reading. For example, lessons might focus on how to recognize and orally interpret punctuation (e.g., the falling pitch and pause that accompany a period at the end of a sentence, the rising pitch and pause that accompany a question mark at the end of a sentence, the brief pause that accompanies a comma, and the stress or emphasis that accompanies italicized or bold typeface). Opitz and Rasinski (1998) refer to this type of activity as "Look for the Signals."

Lessons might also focus on teaching the characteristics of fluent reading (e.g., reading smoothly, reading steadily, reading with few pauses, reading accurately, and reading with expression). Providing students with good models of fluent oral reading during your read-aloud sessions will help them learn what fluent reading sounds like. However, many children will not be able to internalize the features of fluent oral reading simply by listening. Thus, you will also need to provide some mini-lessons in which you teach children about its characteristics. For example, if you were trying to teach students to read smoothly, you might demonstrate how the same sentence or paragraph would sound if you read it very smoothly (as if conversing with another person), moderately smoothly (some parts were conversational and some were choppy), and choppy. Have students listen to and rate which version of your reading was smoothest. Follow your demonstrations with a discussion, and then have students chorally read the same sentence, paragraph, rhyme, or poem with you again so they can hear how smooth reading sounds.

After your lesson, plan activities that enable children to practice reading and rereading the text over and over to develop fluency. Children should practice rereading the text (or their portion of the text) a specified number of times or until they have reached a specified level of proficiency. You can use activities such as partner reading, in which students select a piece of text (or a poem, song lyric, rhyme, etc.) to read together. It is important to show students how, with practice, their smoothness (or the feature on which you are working) improves. To accomplish this, students should continually evaluate their own reading and rereading (see Figure 3.8). Children might also elect to practice fluency at a listening center at which they record their readings and rereadings, play them back, and use the evaluation to rate their smoothness as they listen. Over time and with each rereading, students can compare their current rereading to their first reading to illustrate how practice helps fluency. After children have learned about all of the features of fluent oral reading, they can evaluate their rereading, using a form similar to that in Figure 3.9.

After students have reached the desired level of fluency or proficiency, pairs or small groups can share their accomplishments through dramatic readings or performances. By performances we do not mean large-scale productions accompanied by props, backdrops, and costumes, but rather simple, modest ways of sharing students' accomplishments. Worthy and Prater (2002) remind us that these brief performances can take place every week and may not run smoothly at first. Over time, as students plan, practice, and perform on a number of occasions, you can work with them to establish routines and appropriate behavior. Students may perform for one another, parents, or small groups of younger children.

Shared reading need not be done with patterned, predictable texts or with narratives, which some children may not enjoy. Children who prefer informational texts may practice rereading books designed to inform others about particular topics or current events. Rather than performing what they have practiced as a drama, these students may create their own weekly news program in which they gather information about current events, write their own stories, and practice rereading them for a classwide, gradewide, or schoolwide news program.

Types of Shared Reading Activities

Numerous types of shared reading activities provide practice in becoming fluent (see Opitz & Rasinski, 1998). Four activities that are simple to plan and implement with third graders include (1) Buddy/Partner Reading, (2) choral reading, (3) Readers' Theater, and (4) books on tape. In *Buddy/Partner Reading*, two chil-

Name: _____

Date: _____

Text: _____

Page(s): _____

Reading #____	My reading was:	Very smooth	Mostly smooth	A little smooth	Not smooth
Reading #____	My reading was:	Very smooth	Mostly smooth	A little smooth	Not smooth
Reading #____	My reading was:	Very smooth	Mostly smooth	A little smooth	Not smooth
Reading #____	My reading was:	Very smooth	Mostly smooth	A little smooth	Not smooth
Reading #____	My reading was:	Very smooth	Mostly smooth	A little smooth	Not smooth
Reading #____	My reading was:	Very smooth	Mostly smooth	A little smooth	Not smooth
Reading #____	My reading was:	Very smooth	Mostly smooth	A little smooth	Not smooth
Reading #____	My reading was:	Very smooth	Mostly smooth	A little smooth	Not smooth
Reading #____	My reading was:	Very smooth	Mostly smooth	A little smooth	Not smooth

FIGURE 3.8. Self-evaluation of smoothness.

Name: _____

Text: _____

Date: _____

	Not at All	Some of the Time	Most of the Time	All of the Time
I read smoothly.				
I read at a steady pace.				
I had short pauses between the words when I read.				
My reading was accurate.				
My reading had expression.				
I used the punctuation marks to help make my reading more expressive.				

I worked really hard to _____

Next time I will _____

FIGURE 3.9. Self-evaluation of fluency.

dren practice reading their text simultaneously. After each rereading, the buddies reflect on their rendition and evaluate themselves verbally or with a self-evaluation form similar to those in Figures 3.8 and 3.9.

In *choral reading*, groups of children read the selected text orally together. Poems, chants, and rhymes are particularly good for choral reading. The group's goal is to create an interpretation of the text that conveys its spirit and mood. Chorally reciting the Pledge of Allegiance is one example (as long as children can see a copy of the text; otherwise it is considered memorization rather than shared reading). Paul Fleischman's *Joyful Noise: Poems for Two Voices* (1988) is an excellent choice for choral reading because each poem was written to be read aloud by two readers (or groups of readers) simultaneously, with one group reading the left-hand side of the page and the other reading the right. When both parts are read chorally, the poem takes on the quality of a duet. Beyond the benefit of developing fluency, choral reading gives children who may be shy or reluctant to read aloud the support of the entire group (Opitz & Rasinski, 1998).

In *Readers' Theater*, various members of the class or even the entire class performs a story or script. Unlike a play, Readers' Theater does not require students to memorize their lines. They have the script in front of them as they perform, which is why it is an example of shared reading. The performance does not require props, backdrops, or costumes. Stories that lend themselves to Readers' Theater are those in which there are several characters and/or a narrator. Nearly any piece of children's literature can be transformed into a Readers' Theater script. While working as a reading specialist, I (JFA) had the opportunity to work with a small group of struggling second-grade readers. We were reading *Sir Small and the Dragonfly* (1988) by Jane O'Connor, which the group thought would make an excellent play. As with most open-ended tasks selected by students, the group's motivation was endless. Together we reread the text over and over again and discussed what a script might look like; that is, as we reread the text we talked about how the author lets readers know who is speaking. We began a shared writing activity in which we transformed the book into a script by examining the characters and determining which parts of the text should be spoken by each character. As we reread, the group noted that some parts of the text, outside of the characters, also provided information. This became a perfect opportunity to teach the group about narrators.

As the script came to life, students began to "audition" for desired roles. One student was particularly introverted and shy. I felt the part of Sir Small, the hero of the story, was perfect for him for several reasons. First, it was a small role in that Sir Small actually had few speaking parts (much of his character was communicated through the narrator), and I felt the honor of playing the hero might help this child's low self-esteem, which was evident primarily in his spoken language: He mumbled when he spoke and, even after multiple rereadings, held his hand over his mouth as he read his lines. With each day's rereading, these readers, many of whom were tentative and disfluent, became more confident—even our leading man, Sir Small. Ultimately Readers' Theater gave these students an outlet for expressing their interpretation of the text through a dramatic rereading, provided a wonderful opportunity to enhance every student's fluency, and built much needed self-esteem and motivation for reading.

Books on tape is an activity in which a fluent oral reading is available on an audiocassette, a CD, or online. Many books on tape feature professional actors. However, if your budget is limited, you might ask parent volunteers to make tapes to accompany texts, or you might ask an older class in your school to tape fluent oral readings for your class. The books and the tapes can be placed at a listening center, where students can select a text and listen to it being read aloud as they follow along. To truly be a shared reading rather than a read-aloud, students should try to read along with the tape.

Teacher-Guided Reading Instruction

Entire books are dedicated to the topic of guided reading instruction (e.g., Fountas & Pinnell, 1996) and strategy instruction (e.g., Almasi, 2003). Guided reading instruction is a complicated topic; therefore, the purpose of this section is merely to introduce you to its primary components.

What Is Teacher-Guided Reading and Why Is It Important?

Teacher-guided reading instruction is the portion of your reading program in which you give your students explicit instruction to enhance their reading abilities. Reading experts define guided reading in many ways. To Tompkins and McGee (1993, pp. 20–21) it is an approach in which the teacher directs readers' attention toward "events, vocabulary, the author's craft, a genre, or an author's style." The teachers may ask questions, make predictions, discuss the reading, or share insights with the students. Fountas and Pinnell (1996, p. 2) have defined guided reading as "a context in which a teacher supports each reader's development of effective strategies for processing novel texts at increasingly challenging levels of difficulty." Guided reading for Fountas and Pinnell involves working with a small group of students as they read a text at their instructional level. The teacher introduces the text to the students, observes and interacts with the children as they read, and explains one or two "teaching points" after they have finished. Students may also participate in an extension of their reading. Overall the goal of guided reading is to enable students to learn to use strategies independently. Fountas and Pinnell's text provides a wonderful overview of how to implement guided reading. However, for the purpose of this book, we will call this instructional component of a balanced literacy program teacher-guided reading to distinguish it from other models.

The goal of teacher-guided reading is to give students instruction that enables them to read successfully on their own, usually at their instructional reading level. Books at this level offer some challenges in word identification or comprehension, but they are not so difficult that they would frustrate the child. Therefore, with some instruction, the student will be able to read the book. Books at a student's frustration level are not recommended for guided instruction. Instead, you might use them in a read-aloud or recommend that parents or guardians read to the child at home.

Teacher-guided reading instruction is essential in helping students progress to higher levels of reading ability and become self-regulated, independent readers. Although a few children may be able to learn to read on their own with little support or guidance, most children require some form of instructional support. As noted in Chapter 2, by third grade most children will be fairly good readers in terms of their ability to recognize unknown words and to comprehend. However, teacher-guided reading instruction will help them move beyond these basic levels of literacy.

Durkin's (1978/79) research found that much of the time spent in literacy classrooms was devoted to "mentioning" (mentioning the skill students were supposed to practice), "practicing" (i.e., practicing the skill), and "assessing" (giving directions to complete assignments and workbook pages), but little time was actually spent on teaching students *how* to understand and comprehend text. Because of Durkin's landmark study, researchers in the 1980s began to examine whether more concerted efforts to provide explicit instruction would enhance students' learning and their strategic and metacognitive awareness—particularly for struggling readers. These studies found, in general, that when students were given explicit instruction that included explanation, modeling, and guided practice, their comprehension was enhanced (e.g., Dole, Brown, & Trathen, 1996; Duffy et al., 1987). Despite the significant effects on students' learning, researchers are finding that little explicit comprehension instruction still occurs in elementary classrooms (Fielding & Pearson, 1994; Pearson & Dole, 1987; Pearson & Fielding, 1991; Pearson & Gallagher, 1983; Pressley, 2000).

During teacher-guided reading instruction, the teacher has objectives and goals for the lesson and provides explanation, modeling, and guided practice to attain them. Such explanations must go beyond "mentioning" and focus on *what* strategy is being used, *what* knowledge is associated with the strategy, *why* it is being used in a given situation, *why* it is helpful in that situation, *when* the strategy can be used, and *how* to perform the strategy. Over time, the teacher gradually releases responsibility for directing the instruction to the students until they are capable of engaging in the process on their own (Pearson & Gallagher, 1983).

Teacher-guided reading instruction of strategies should not occur in isolation, without connected text, or as distinct and separate activities (Pearson & Dole, 1987). It must be embedded within and linked to authentic reading events. Teachers must be attuned to the learning environment so they are able to identify opportune moments in which to insert "strategy language" and provide opportunities for students to engage in similar language use. These opportunities for student verbalization and dialogue about strategy enables students to try out, or appropriate, strategy language for their own use (Almasi, 2003).

What Does Teacher-Guided Reading Instruction Look Like in Third Grade?

The first step in planning teacher-guided reading instruction involves assessing your students to determine their strengths and challenges as readers. We will examine such assessment thoroughly in Chapter 4. Although no two children in your class will have the same goals, some children may have similar goals in word identification, comprehension, vocabulary development, or interpretive strategies. Thus, you may be able to create small groups to accommodate various instructional needs. These groups need not be static. That is, you can (and should) continually group and regroup your students to match their instructional goals. Very often the number of groups may range from two to four at any given time, with the number of children in each group ranging from one to eight. If there are any more than eight in a group, however, it will be difficult to meet the individual needs of each child. Therefore, you should keep the groups as small as possible. Although many models of guided reading instruction recommend placing students in groups based on reading levels, we are recommending the practice of flexible grouping (Flood, Lapp, Flood, & Nagel, 1992). Serious social problems can arise for students when they are placed in ability groups, leading to cognitive problems over time.

In the effort to avoid ability grouping, however, many teachers move to the other end of the spectrum—whole-class instruction. This is not recommended either, as it does not provide the requisite level of individualization (a point that will be examined in more detail in Chapter 6). It is completely unlikely that you would ever have an entire class of third graders all reading at the same level, with identical word identification needs, identical comprehension needs, identical vocabulary needs, identical interests, and identical levels of motivation.

In flexible grouping, children are grouped and regrouped continually throughout the year, based on a variety of factors. For example, you might group students according to awareness and use of word identification or comprehension strategies, prior knowledge of content, prior knowledge of strategies, interest, social factors, or student choice (Flood et al., 1992). Groups may comprise individuals, dyads, small groups (3–6), or larger groups (7–8). Texts may be flexible as well; at times you may use the same text with all of your groups, you may use texts of varying reading levels with different groups, or you may use texts with different themes but similar topics with each group. The key is to remain flexible throughout the year to meet the changing instructional needs and interests of your students.

HOW DO I PLAN FOR TEACHER-GUIDED READING?

Once you have grouped your students and selected your materials, you must plan your instructional goals and objectives for each group. These should be based on students' needs, but as noted in Chapter 2, we generally have some idea of the types of lessons most third graders might need at some point throughout the year. Tompkins and McGee (1993) suggest that the instructional program itself be balanced in terms of what is actually taught during teacher-guided instruction. They include three programmatic aspects: the "interactive" perspective, the "critical" perspective, and the "reader response" perspective. The interactive perspective involves instructing children how to process text strategically. This means teaching students to use word identification strategies to recognize unknown words, comprehension strategies to make sense of the texts, and interpretive strategies to come to deeper insights regarding their interpretations. Figure 3.10 displays strategies you might include in your teacher-guided reading instruction when teaching from an interactive perspective.

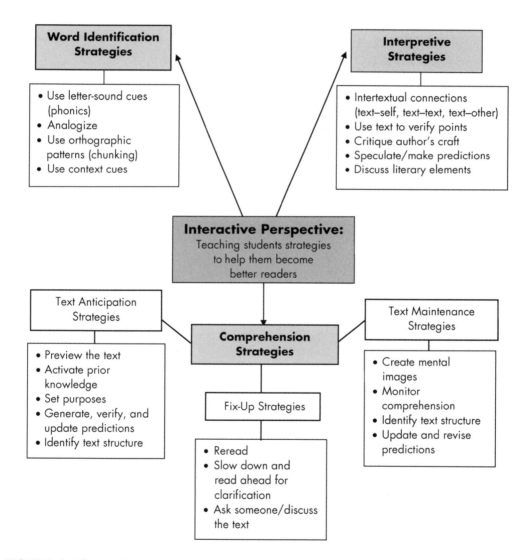

FIGURE 3.10. Goals and objectives for teacher-guided reading instruction from an interactive perspective.

When teaching from the critical perspective, teachers show students how to understand the ways in which authors craft various texts. As depicted in Figure 3.11, these lessons focus on how narrative text (prose) is structured, how expository texts are structured, the author's style/craft, and genre. Students learn to recognize and understand the structures underlying texts, which helps them not only as readers but also as writers. Third graders learn to identify the structures and attach literary labels to them. If such instruction is linked to writing, third graders

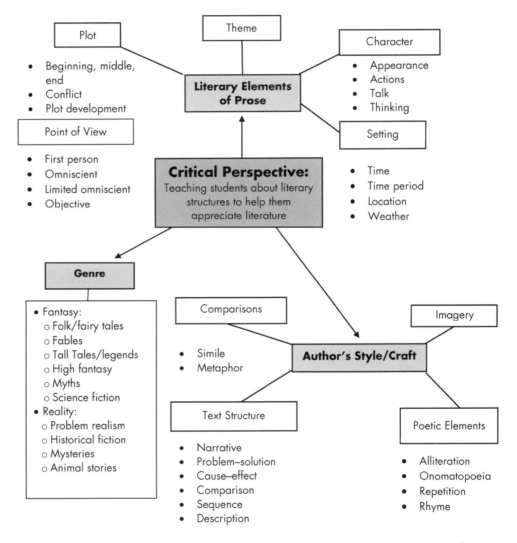

FIGURE 3.11. Goals and objectives for teacher-guided reading instruction from a critical perspective.

become more proficient writers because they understand how authors create such texts and can then use the underlying structures to guide their own writing. Thus, it is important to provide instruction related not only to how to read (strategy) but also how to appreciate literature.

Finally, students should learn to read and respond to text aesthetically. They should select texts, read them, and respond to them in some manner (e.g., artistic, dramatic, and written responses), but their responses should not be graded. The responses should come from within and should represent the students' innermost thoughts, expressions, or feelings. Overall, then, as you plan your instructional program, you must balance these three perspectives: interactive, critical, and reader response.

HOW DO I IMPLEMENT TEACHER-GUIDED READING INSTRUCTION?

The final aspect of teacher-guided reading instruction is actually implementing it. Because you will need to work with each small group, the other groups must be self-directed for a portion of the guided reading time. Therefore, it is helpful to establish routines and expectations during teacher-guided reading instruction. The routine can certainly vary, but it is good to have a general plan for the duration of each component. For example, if you have a 90-minute literacy block, you might plan it in a manner similar to that depicted in Figure 3.12.

Suppose your entire class was fairly unaware of expository text structures. At the start of your literacy block, you might plan a 15-minute mini-lesson in which you explain what compare/contrast text structure is and how authors use cue words to communicate similarities and differences. The objective would be for stu-

Time	Group 1	Group 2	Group 3
9:00–9:15	Whole class mini-lesson on compare/contrast text structure		
9:15–9:30	Teacher read-aloud		
9:30–9:50	Meets with teacher for guided reading instruction	Works independently on reading/writing (guided practice)	Works in learning centers
9:50–10:10	Works independently on reading/writing (guided practice)	Works in learning centers	Meets with teacher for guided reading instruction
10:10–10:30	Works in learning centers	Meets with teacher for guided reading instruction	Works independently on reading/writing (guided practice)

FIGURE 3.12. Sample schedule for a 90-minute literacy block featuring teacher-guided reading instruction.

dents to be able to identify cue words that indicate compare/contrast structure. In your mini-lesson, you might activate prior knowledge by having students brainstorm the similarities and differences between frogs and toads. You can record their thoughts on a piece of chart paper or a white board so they can refer to these ideas later. At this point, you could also quickly remind students how important it is to activate our prior knowledge before reading any text. This will help them see how to transfer strategy knowledge to all reading contexts (you will also be modeling what good strategy users do every time they read text of any type). You can also use the list of similarities and differences to explain the use of cue words to help communicate clearly. Some words and phrases that communicate similarity are *same, similar, also, and, too,* and *all.* Words and phrases that communicate difference include *different, but, in contrast,* and *on the other hand.* You could then use the list of similarities to model how you might write a sentence describing similar features of frogs and toads and a sentence describing differences. Students can then work with a partner to write one or two other sentences that describe similarities and differences between frogs and toads. In this way you have provided a brief explanation of the compare/contrast text structure and what cue words indicate it, modeled how authors use the cue words to communicate similarity and difference, and provided some brief guided practice.

Following the mini-lesson, you could read aloud a text that has the compare/contrast structure. In Kalman and Evert's (1994) *Frogs and Toads,* the similarities and differences between frogs and toads are examined in relation to their characteristics, habitats, diet, and life cycle. Using this expository text as a read-aloud not only reinforces compare/contrast text structure and introduces your students to a different genre but also enables them to hear fluent oral reading from an expository text. You may not want to read all of the text during this read-aloud session because you might stop at various places to point out some of the cue words the author uses to highlight similarity and difference. Kalman and Everts use some cue words explicitly to indicate compare/contrast text structure, as in the sentence "Frogs *and* toads belong to a group of animals called amphibians" (p. 4). They also use explicit cue words to indicate similarity and difference: "Frogs and toads look *similar, but* they are different in some ways" (p. 7). You might give the students cards cue words and ask them to hold up the cue word when they hear it during the read-aloud. When they hold up a given cue card, you could stop to informally assess which students were able to recognize it and which were not. You could then use that time to discuss whether the cue word helped communicate the information more clearly. After reading, students can update or revise the information they brainstormed earlier to reflect the new content they learned from the read-aloud.

After the mini-lesson and read-aloud, students would break into their flexible groups (see Figure 3.12). While you are meeting with group 1, group 2 is working independently on a reading and writing follow-up assignment from the mini-lesson. This assignment might require the group to work as a whole, or pairs of students to work together, to update the prior knowledge chart and use the information therein to write a paragraph describing how frogs and toads are similar and different. When the group finishes this assignment, the students can move to a learning center of their choice. While group 2 is engaged in the writing assignment, students in group 3 are at the learning centers. By having groups use centers at different points in the literacy block, you keep them from vying for a limited number of spaces.

During teacher-guided reading lessons for each group, you could select other expository texts with a compare/contrast structure; however, the texts should have different topics and different reading levels to address students' individual needs. From your earlier assessments, for example, you found that the children you placed in group 1 had difficulty in reading polysyllabic words. Those children in group 2 were able to read polysyllabic words fairly well and were fairly fluent readers; however, they have had little exposure to expository texts and need additional instruction related to text structure. The students in group 3 were at a more emergent level. Like group 1 they were having difficulty in reading polysyllabic words; however, they were also having difficulty in monitoring their comprehension. Although you have selected expository texts for each group, the accompanying lessons will vary, based on students' needs. All of the lessons you plan for teacher-guided reading instruction that day involved teaching about word identification strategies and strategies to identify and use text structure. Therefore, they are from the interactive perspective (see Figure 3.10). For balance, you will want to provide lessons from the critical perspective, as well as time for students to respond aesthetically to the texts later on in the week.

During your lessons, you have selected a portion of the text for children to read silently while they are with you. Before reading, of course, you will want to introduce the selection and encourage students to use text anticipation strategies, such as previewing the text, activating prior knowledge, and setting purposes. You may want to brainstorm and record prior knowledge on a chart for all students to see, or you may have students brainstorm on their own and record their purpose for reading in a journal or on a blank bookmark. You will also want to provide an explanation of the strategy on which you are focusing and model how to use it before the children read (see Almasi, 2003, for further information about strategy instruction and sample lesson plans). In this way, you are preparing students to be more successful as they read the text silently.

After your explanation and modeling, you provide time for students to practice using the strategies you have just taught by having them read a portion of the text. As they are reading, you might ask them to note where, when, and why they used the strategy on which you are focusing (see Figure 4.7 for a sample chart to use with chunking). As students read, you may use the time to make anecdotal notes of whether they are using the strategy you have taught, you might pull one student aside and have him or her read the text aloud to you as a running record of the student's reading, or you might use the time to circulate among the students who are working independently or in small groups around the room.

After students have finished reading, the postreading discussion might focus on how well the strategy worked. It is critical for *students* to have time to talk about when and where they used the strategy and how well it worked for them (Almasi, 2003). Thus, you might pose an open-ended question, such as "So tell me how you used the chunking strategy we learned about before we read?" From there students can engage in a conversation about the strategy. The postreading discussion might also be an opportunity to highlight the content in terms of how well the author communicated similarities and differences in the text. This discussion need not be directed or guided by you. Students can easily engage in their own peer discussions of text (see Gambrell & Almasi, 1996). While students are discussing these topics, you might use the time to quickly circulate about the room to check on the other students. Upon your return to the group, the students can update you.

All these activities cannot occur in a 20-minute lesson, but the ideas are presented to show an instructional sequence that might occur with this group across several days as they learn about the strategy, read the text, and discuss it.

Independent Reading

What Is Independent Reading?

Independent reading is another vital component in a balanced literacy program. The independent reading portion enables readers to select texts to read on their own. These should be texts in which the students are highly interested, motivated to read, and capable of reading on their own. The texts should not be at the students' frustrational or even their instructional level. Students should be able to read the text independently. That is, they should be able to read nearly all of the words accurately (about 99%), and their comprehension should be high.

The type of texts children select for independent reading should not be of concern. Sometimes teachers are fearful children will not read novels if they are allowed to read magazines, comic books, or series books for independent reading. The time to introduce children to book-length novels and chapter books is during the read-aloud and guided reading portions of your literacy program. During independent reading, children should be permitted to read whatever they want. What they read is unimportant as long as they spend time reading for fun. There is no expectation for any accountability following the reading. That is, there are no book reports, no response journal entries, no written summaries, and there are absolutely no questions to answer either orally, in writing, or on a computer (as in Accelerated Reader programs). The goal of independent reading is pure enjoyment.

Why Is Independent Reading Important?

Research has consistently shown that students read only between 8 and 15 minutes per day in school (Taylor, Frye, & Maruyama, 1990). These numbers are shocking, given that many elementary classrooms dedicate as much as 90 minutes per day to literacy instruction. Yet somehow during that time students do very little authentic reading.

Krashen (2004, p. 1) examined the research literature concerning what he referred to as "free voluntary reading" (i.e., independent reading). Although he recognized that independent reading by itself will not lead to higher levels of reading proficiency, he noted that it "provides a foundation so that higher levels of proficiency may be reached." Krashen's review of 54 studies found that in 51 (94%) of the studies, students who participated in independent reading programs fared as well or better on reading tests than their counterparts who participated in traditional skills-based programs without independent reading. That is, students who participated in independent reading had "better reading comprehension, writing style, vocabulary, spelling, and grammatical development" (p. 17). Moreover, the longer independent reading is done (minutes per day), the more consistently positive the results. Thus, giving students the opportunity to engage in independent reading on a daily basis is another critical component of your third-grade literacy program.

How Do I Fit Independent Reading into the Literacy Program?

There are many ways to find time for independent reading. One way is to initiate a common time each day in which the entire class (including the teacher) engages in independent reading. In some classrooms, this is called Sustained Silent Reading (SSR), Drop Everything and Read (DEAR), or self-selected reading. Some schools engage in a schoolwide independent reading time in which all staff members (including administrators, faculty, staff, and students) literally drop everything and read for a given time each day, perhaps for 10–20 minutes. Schoolwide or classroom common times for independent reading communicate the value of reading for pleasure. When each individual in the school or the classroom sets aside their "business" to make time for pleasure reading, students soon realize the importance of the event. During this time, teachers should not be grading papers or monitoring students' reading. It is purely a time in which everyone reads for pleasure.

Some schools and classrooms are unable (or unwilling) to devote a common time for independent reading. In these situations, you can find time throughout your day to encourage students to read independently. For example, your morning message each day may direct students to either the classroom library or the school library to select a book for independent reading and then to begin reading it. In this way, students will not waste precious minutes intended for independent reading on selecting a text. You may also find time during your literacy block to include 10–15 minutes of classwide independent reading, or you may encourage students to read independently during the learning center portion of your teacher-guided reading instruction.

Although most third graders will be able to read independently for 15–20 minutes or longer, some students have difficulty in engaging in independent reading for a sustained period of time. For these students, you may want to begin with a brief period of time, say, 5 minutes. Then each week you can add 1 minute to the period to gradually build up the ability to engage in sustained independent reading. It is also helpful to have a precise time limit, so setting a timer aids in structuring the period. An essential rule for independent reading is that the time should be spent on *reading*, not selecting, books. Thus, students should already have a text for independent reading before it begins. Some students need guidance in selecting a text that is interesting and motivating and can be read on their own (as described in Chapter 2). A lesson on how to select books or use the five-finger rule could make an excellent 15-minute whole-class mini-lesson at the beginning of one of the teacher-guided reading lessons in September.

SUMMARY

Creating a space in which children are motivated to read is one of the most important goals for literacy instruction in third grade. This space should reflect your pedagogical beliefs, values, and philosophy through (1) the instructional materials and texts you place in your classroom, (2) the way in which you physically arrange those materials and the furniture in your room, (3) your own demeanor, and (4) the instructional program you establish for literacy. The literacy program, in particular, should be balanced to include teacher read-alouds, shared reading, teacher-guided reading instruction, and independent reading each day. Instruction should come from an interactive perspective in which children learn to use a variety of word identification, comprehension, and interpretive strategies for making sense of text. Instruction should also focus at times on critical perspectives in which children are taught to understand and appreciate how texts are crafted and structured. Finally, the instructional program should provide time in which children are able to read and respond to text aesthetically, without any form of evaluation.

CHAPTER 4

GETTING TO KNOW YOUR STUDENTS VIA CLASSROOM ASSESSMENT

WHAT IS CLASSROOM ASSESSMENT?

Assessments enable teachers to determine how well students understand content, respond to lessons, and are motivated or interested. Classroom assessment enables teachers not only to understand students but also to refine and make adjustments to the lessons taught and to the instructional programs planned.

Carlisle and Rice (2004) identified four purposes for assessments of reading. One purpose involves program evaluation and accountability. In general, these assessments are designed at district and state levels and are used by administrators and policymakers as a means of holding schools and teachers accountable for reading progress. Calfee and Hiebert (1991) refer to this as "formal" assessment. It is formal in that it is designed for external accountability. Scores on such assessments are a single index of student achievement that stands apart from curriculum and instruction. These assessments are often objective, standardized measures that provide comparisons of an individual student's score in relation to a normed sample (e.g., California Achievement Test, Terra Nova, and Woodcock–Johnson Reading Mastery test). These tests usually have a multiple-choice format and include subtests of word attack, comprehension, and vocabulary. Formal assessments of reading are primarily concerned with the products of reading. That is, they are concerned with how well a student performs in relation to others at the same age level.

A second purpose for assessment is to identify those children who may have special needs in reading (Carlisle & Rice, 2004). Usually this type of assessment is used to determine whether students who are experiencing difficulty in learning to read and write qualify for special education services. Specific criteria for identifying such learning disabilities are established by federal law.

A third purpose for assessment is to identify students who are at risk for learning problems (Carlisle & Rice, 2004). The goal of this assessment is to provide appropriate interventions in time to prevent any serious difficulty in acquiring literacy.

A fourth purpose for assessment is to monitor student progress in reading and use this information to evaluate, refine, and modify classroom instruction (Carlisle & Rice, 2004). Calfee and Hiebert (1991) classify this form of assessment as "informal." Informal assessments are typically developed by classroom teachers, strongly linked to curriculum and instruction, and intended to be used in the classroom. They include performance-based and authentic assessments of literacy such as observations, interviews, informal reading inventories, miscue analyses, and discussion. These assessments can be used with the whole class, small groups, or individual students. Rather than comparing scores of students to one another, as in formal assessments, the goal of informal assessment is to *inform* instruction so that students attain higher levels of literacy. Thus, these informal assessments of students' reading should be used in conjunction with instruction so that assessment and instruction inform one another. In this manner, assessment is not an end product to evaluate student performance. Instead, it is a critical component of the instructional process that helps teachers plan, evaluate, and modify their instruction on a continual basis. It is this final purpose that is most useful and viable for classroom teachers. Thus, the remainder of this chapter will focus on explanations and descriptions of classroom-based assessments of reading for evaluating and modifying your classroom instruction.

How Can I Use Assessment to Inform Instruction?

Assessments used to inform instruction are not only informal but also formative in the sense of indicating progress toward educational goals and objectives (Carlisle & Rice, 2004). In other words, the data you gather on a daily basis through informal, formative assessments should help you plan future lessons to meet students' needs. Such assessments enable you to be *responsive* to your students, that is, to be attentive and reactive to their cognitive, social, and motivational needs. You are also able to reflect on the strengths and weaknesses of each lesson and how students responded to it. The data gathered in this ongoing manner will help you determine how best to teach your students.

Klenk and Almasi (1997) developed a model of ongoing assessment based on the work of Gillett and Temple (1994). A simplified version is shown in Figure 4.1. The three components of ongoing assessment include (1) observing and assessing students; (2) planning and implementing instruction with students; and (3) generating, revising, or deleting hypotheses about students. The ongoing assessment

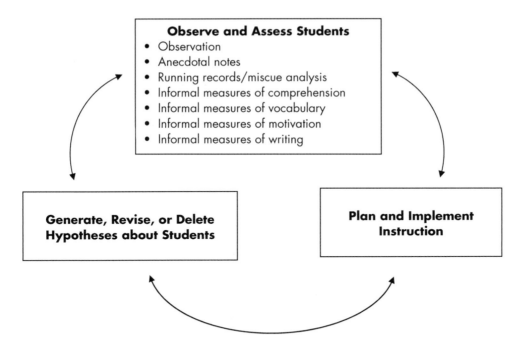

FIGURE 4.1. Model of ongoing assessment and instruction. Adapted from Klenk and Almasi (1997). Copyright 1997 by the New York State Reading Association. Adapted by permission.

process can begin at any point in the cycle. Often you will begin by teaching a lesson, observing your students to see how they respond to it. Your reflections on the lesson and your observations will help you determine the effectiveness of your instruction. You can also generate hypotheses about your students' strengths and challenges based on that instruction. Instruction without assessment makes it impossible to evaluate its effectiveness. If the ongoing assessment cycle does not include generating or revising or deleting hypotheses about your students' strengths and challenges as readers, you will not know how to adjust future lessons to meet their individual needs. Thus, ongoing assessment is a recursive process in which all components are integral and inform one another.

TYPES OF CLASSROOM ASSESSMENTS IN LITERACY

When we think of assessment, we often think of written assessment. In the classroom, informal assessments of comprehension often consist of literal and inferential questions in which children write "answers" derived from their understanding of the text. Traditional classroom assessments of word recognition often consist of worksheets in which children are asked to circle items exhibiting a particular vowel or consonant sound. The most typical classroom assessment of vocabulary requires students to locate and write definitions of vocabulary words from the dictionary. If we are truly attempting to create a third-grade classroom environment that fosters literacy and motivation for reading, these types of assessments are not the answer. Instead, let's envision assessments in a different way—those that children are anxious to undertake and be part of, rather than those that children approach with dread, apathy, or anxiety. Let's envision assessments that tell us a great deal about the way children think while they are reading, rather than those that tell us whether children are "right" or "wrong." In short, let's envision alternatives to traditional classroom assessments of reading and writing, as examined in this section.

When I (JFA) began teaching I was fortunate to be in a district that would not allow worksheets, dittoes, or workbook pages to be used to assess students on a daily basis. Challenging as this was, it forced me to be resourceful and creative in designing daily assessments for my students. The benefits, however, were enormous. My students enjoyed the assessments and actually looked forward to them, while I learned a great deal about the processes my students used to read and make sense of text.

The assessment tasks we design for our third graders should promote open-ended inquiry and provide insight into the *processes* students use when they read. If you are able to understand and gain insight into this process, you are better able to help them grow. For example, if a child answers several comprehension questions "incorrectly," all you know is that he does not understand the text. You do not know *why* he did not understand, and you do not understand what his thinking was while he was reading. Likewise, drill and skill worksheets designed to assess a student's understanding of vowel sounds only tell you whether she can identify vowel sounds in isolation. It does not provide information about whether she is able to use letters and the sounds they make to help her read unknown words.

Like the tasks we design for our centers, the tasks we design and use for classroom assessments should be open-ended, challenging, and allow for student choice (Turner, 1995). These tasks will enhance student motivation for reading and yield a plethora of rich data. Where possible, we should also endeavor to assess the *process* of reading, rather than the *products* of reading. The descriptions that follow provide a variety of ways to assess your students' reading processes.

Conversation

Responsive teaching requires awareness of the specific needs of each individual student and the contexts that yield optimal learning (Pressley & Afflerbach, 1995). Very often such information is not evident in written assessments or observations, although informal conversations can provide such insight (Lipson, 1996). Informal conversations can occur at any time or in any place, for example, while students are selecting texts for independent reading or working on a project. These conversations might consist of simple queries, such as "Wow, I'm glad to see you're choosing a book for silent reading time! Why did you pick that one?" or "What do you enjoy about that author's books?" Thus you gain insight into a student's motivation for reading and ability level. Without asking why a student selected a particular book, all you know is what book he or she chose; you do not understand the rationale for the selection. Some examples of conversational interviews include metacognitive and book interviews.

Metacognitive Interviews

Metacognitive interviews are designed to help you understand how your students think about their own reading processes. Almasi (2003) explains that such interviews can be used to gain insights into students' perceptions about reading, the strategies they believe they use to read unknown words and make sense of text, their preferences while reading, and the values and beliefs they have about reading. Although metacognitive interviews could be administered to the entire class as a written survey, Almasi does not recommend that they be used in this manner. As noted in Chapter 1, third graders are increasingly metacognitive about their own abilities; however, many may not be fully aware of the processes they use while they are reading. If they are required to think about the way they read, while reading questions about reading, while writing . . . and so on, they may be on cognitive (and metacognitive) overload. Also, some third graders may limit the information they give you if they are expected to write. For example, they may not be motivated to include all the strategic processing they really do while reading if they have to write it all down. They may be inhibited or anxious about their inability to spell particular words and so opt to write something less accurate rather than risk misspelling a word or taking the time to write about all of the things they really do. In short, it is easier for third graders to talk about the processes they use while reading than for them to write about them. Thus, you will gain more accurate information by having informal conversations with students individually. A metacognitive interview is shown in Figure 4.2. These questions are only examples. You will want to select those that best fit your needs and add additional questions as necessary.

Text Interviews

Text interviews are another way to gather information through conversation about your students' interests, their perceptions of their reading ability, and the way they approach text. To prepare for a text interview, you should select a number of texts, representing a wide variety of topics, genres, and readability levels (Almasi, 2003). These texts need not be exclusively "books" and should include narrative and informational texts, magazines, newspapers, CD liner notes, texts downloaded from the Internet (or available to read on a computer), and so on. The broader the

1. When you are reading, what do you do when you come to something you don't know?
    a. What do you do when you read something that doesn't make sense?
    b. What do you do when you come to a word you don't know?

2. Which do you like best, reading out loud or to yourself? Why?

3. Which do you think takes longer, reading out loud or reading silently? Why?

4. What types of things does your teacher have you do during reading time?

5. Do you like to read? Why or why not?

6. Do you read at home? How often?
    a. Where do you read?
    b. Do you read to yourself or to someone else?
    c. What types of things do you like to read?

7. Let's say the kindergarten teacher has asked you to help her during reading time. How would you teach a kindergarten child how to read?

8. Do you think it's important to know how to read? Why or why not?

9. What is a good reader? How could you be a better reader?

10. Do you ever read anything easy in school? If so, what?

FIGURE 4.2. Sample metacognitive interview. Developed by Beth Davey, University of Maryland.

From Almasi (2003, p. 30). Copyright 2003 by The Guilford Press. Reprinted with permission in *Teaching Literacy in Third Grade* by Janice F. Almasi, Keli Garas-York, and Leigh-Ann Hildreth. Permission to photocopy this figure is granted to purchasers of this book for personal use only (see copyright page for details).

selection of texts, the better you will be able to determine your students' interests, motivations, and attitudes toward reading. The texts should be arranged and displayed in a visually attractive manner so students can see and handle them. In addition, you might ask the students you are interviewing to bring from home some of their favorite reading matter.

A text interview developed by teachers in their master's program is shown in Figure 4.3. Before engaging in a text interview with your students, you will want to decide which questions, or sets of questions, will provide the most helpful information for planning instruction. You may not have time or want to ask all of the questions. After you have selected the questions, begin the interview by asking students to look over the texts on the table. Be sure students have had ample opportunity to see and examine all of them. Carefully observe the way your students approach and handle the texts. Some third graders "dig" right in and begin opening texts and flipping pages—a sign of an eager reader. Other students may seem more reticent, almost "afraid." These students walk around the table, glancing at the texts but not touching them. They rarely even open them. Instead, they make their selections on the basis of the cover alone. Such observational information is important to capture and record in your notes. As you begin asking students to select texts for various purposes, be sure to ask follow-up questions to elicit further information. That is, you do not need to ask the questions in a listlike, rote manner as they are printed on the page. The text interview is conceived as a "conversation" with your third grader about the texts he or she likes and doesn't like. The questions in Figure 4.3 are just ideas—use a few of them as a means of starting a conversation rather than as a formal interview. Johnston (1997) is an excellent resource to help you make interviews—whether metacognitive or text—more conversational. Be sure to record students' responses to your questions.

Many teachers have difficulty in finding time to gather information from students through individual interviews and conversations, but there are several times in each day to steal a few minutes for them. You might select one child to interview each day while students are entering the room in the morning (see Chapter 5). Rather than meeting with small groups for teacher-guided reading instruction, you might elect to use this time to conduct individual conversations with some students while the other students are in learning centers or working on independent reading and writing. Of course, you would not want to do this on a consistent basis as it would take time away from much needed instruction. However, at the beginning of the year, when you are gathering initial information about your students, you might use these ideas to make time to chat with your third graders individually.

Observation and Anecdotal Notes

Another way to gather information about your students' "literate personalities" is through careful observation and anecdotal note taking, that is, carefully documenting what you observe about your students. You will want to focus on one or two

Provide a selection of varied texts that represent diverse interests, genres, and ability levels.

Interest

1. What types of texts do you like to read?

2. Take a look at these texts. Have you ever read any of them before? If so, which ones? What did you think of them?

3. Do you see anything here that you would like to read? Why or why not?

4. Who are your favorite authors? What do you like about his/her books?

Reading Level

Frustration Level (Read-Aloud)

5. Which text, or what type of text, would you like someone to read to you?

6. What types of texts does your family read to you?

7. Which of these texts would be really hard for you to read? What makes it hard?

8. What do you do when you don't understand what you read?

9. What do you do when you come to a word you don't know?

Instructional Level

10. Which of these texts would you like to read? Which, with a little help, do you think you could read?

(continued)

FIGURE 4.3. Text interview. Developed by Angela Bies, Anita Brocker, Erin David, Renee Danielewicz, Sheila Ewing, Anna Figliomeni, Chastity Flynn, Keli Garas, Renee Guzak, Jill Hatfield, Bob Hirsch, Jennifer Izzo, Krista Jaekle, Eileen Ludwig, Jaime Quackenbush, Mike Rock, Kathy Sadowski, Donna Von Hendy, and Kristin Zahn (Spring 2000).

Independent Level

11. Which of these texts would be easy for you to read on your own? What makes it easy?

12. Which of these texts would you choose to read on your own for fun? Why?

13. Which of these texts would you like to read to a younger child? Why?

14. Which of these texts would you feel comfortable reading in front of your class? Why?

Text Handling/Strategic Awareness

15. How would you go about reading this text?

16. What kinds of things do you do before you start to read?

17. What kinds of things do you do while you are reading to help you read the text?

18. What kinds of things do you do while you are reading to help you understand the text?

19. What kinds of things do you do after you read to help you understand or remember the text?

Purpose of Reading

20. Which of these texts would you use to find facts about _____? How would you go about reading this text?

21. (Select two texts of different genres) What is different about these texts? Which type of text do you prefer? Why?

Characteristics of Strategic Readers

22. Do you know someone who is a good reader? If so, what makes that person a good reader?

23. How do you feel about reading? Why?

24. Is it important to learn to read? Why or why not?

FIGURE 4.3. *(continued)*

students each day as they engage in typical literacy activities during read-alouds, shared reading, guided reading, and independent reading. You will also want to set objectives for your observations. For example, you might focus on motivation, social behaviors, or cognitive abilities. Keep these objectives in mind as you observe students during the activities. You will want to be sure to attend to the manner in which they approach the lesson and/or task and any nonverbal cues they may exhibit as they are engaged in the lesson. Nonverbal cues such as furrowed brows, frowns, inattentiveness, or distractedness may be signs of frustration. As you observe, jot down anecdotal notes describing the behaviors (see Figure 4.4). Some teachers find it hard to find time to record and store anecdotal notes. Almasi (2003) described two methods to alleviate some of this difficulty. You might consider carrying a clipboard with taped-on 3″ × 5″ index cards for each student (see Figure 4.5). As you make an observation about a child, you write the note directly on that child's index card. Keeping the cards attached to the clipboard makes it easy to locate each student, record your notes, and store the information.

Another method teachers find helpful is clipping a sheet of white mailing labels to the clipboard. As the teachers observe, they jot down anecdotal notes on

FIGURE 4.4. Leigh-Ann Hildreth taking anecdotal notes.

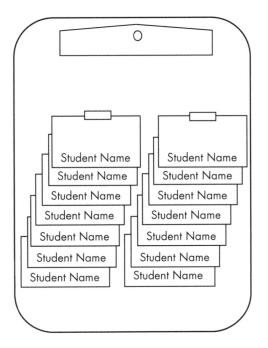

FIGURE 4.5. Using a clipboard to take anecdotal notes of students' performance. From Almasi (2003, p. 23). Copyright 2003 by The Guilford Press. Reprinted by permission.

individual labels for each student. At the end of the day, they peel off and place the labels in each child's folder to make record-keeping quick and easy.

If you are a teacher in a self-contained classroom, it may be difficult to find time to observe and record anecdotal notes. However, if you plan to observe when students are working independently or in small groups, the task will be less burdensome. Team teaching with other grade-level teachers, reading specialists, or special education teachers will also provide situations in which one of the teachers can take observational and anecdotal notes about the students while another is teaching (Klenk & Almasi, 1997).

ASSESSING WORD IDENTIFICATION

Although constructing meaning from text is the primary goal of reading instruction, to do so readers must also be able to recognize and process words fluently (Pressley, 2000; Snow & Sweet, 2003). Word identification for proficient readers is almost always skillful and automatic. These readers rarely need to use strategies to identify words because they are able to recognize automatically nearly all the words they encounter (Almasi, 2003). That is, for proficient readers, nearly all words are sight words—words readers are able to recognize instantly and automatically and do not require analysis or decoding.

At first glance, word identification might appear to be a skillful and automatic process; however, there are times when all readers must approach texts strategically because they cannot decode some of the words. Thus, in learning to identify words and read them fluently, readers must be strategic. For younger and less proficient readers who struggle to identify words, the entire reading process may require strategic processing—in which the reader approaches the task deliberately and planfully (Almasi, 2003)—because they have not attained automaticity. Being strategic is not accidental. When a reader uses a strategy, he or she is deliberate about using it. When readers realize that they do not know how to read a word, they use a word identification strategy to attempt to decode it. Ehri (1991) identifies four strategies readers use, either separately or in combination, to identify unfamiliar words: (1) letter-sound cues, (2) analogues to known words, (3) orthographic features, or (4) context cues. Each strategy is described briefly below. For other strategies and how to teach them, see Fox (2000) or Almasi (2003). When readers use *letter-sound cues* (phonics) to recognize unknown words, they look at the letters in a word, associate sounds with those letters, and use that knowledge to read the words. However, skilled readers do not identify unfamiliar words letter by letter or sound them out letter by letter, as in the letter-sound strategy (Pressley, 2000). As readers mature, they have a store of known words they are able to read by sight, and they are able to recognize common letter patterns in words they do not immediately recognize. Therefore, instead of reading words sequentially in a letter-by-letter fashion, they recognize common letter chunks and blend the chunks together to read unfamiliar words. This makes word recognition a quicker and more automatic process (Ehri, 1991; Fox, 2000). When readers use this *analogizing* strategy to read and identify unknown words, they make use of familiar letter patterns. These letter patterns provide a stable and regular system for decoding. For example, by knowing the -*ank* letter pattern, readers can use that knowledge to read the words *bank, prank,* and *outflank*.

Using *orthographic features*, or chunking, requires recognizing the smaller parts within words to help decode them. Chunking is most helpful with polysyllabic words. Root words, prefixes (e.g., *pre-, un-,* and *dis-*), suffixes (e.g., *-able* and *-or*), contractions (e.g., *isn't* and *wasn't*), and compound words (e.g., *houseboat*) are meaningful multiletter chunks. Meaningful chunks help reveal the meaning of a word and how it might be pronounced. Nonmeaningful multiletter chunks consist of syllables, accents, and other units of pronunciation such as rimes. For example, the word *maple* has two syllables (*ma-* and *-ple*), which do not carry any meaning. They are simply common letter patterns that recur in words. Thus, nonmeaningful chunks help only with sound.

When readers recognize or use the same multiletter chunks repeatedly, in time they internalize these letter patterns and recognize them as intact units. Recognizing multiletter chunks reduces a reader's cognitive burden because it streamlines the word recognition process. When readers decode words letter by letter (as in phonics), they must hold each individual letter sound in their short-term memory (Fox, 2000). When reading longer, polysyllabic words, this becomes an enormous burden. For example, if a reader was trying to pronounce the word *unknowingly* by using the letter-sound strategy, he or she would have to identify and consider 11 individual letters. This overburdens short-term memory, which is only capable of holding between five and seven thought units at one time. When short-term memory is overburdened, some thought units are lost or forgotten. This means that letters at the beginning of the word may be forgotten by the time the entire word has been sounded out, negatively affecting comprehension. If readers can recognize a group of letters as a whole chunk, word recognition becomes more efficient. In the previous example, if the reader used orthographic features to identify the prefix *un-* as one multiletter chunk, the root word *know* as another chunk, and the suffixes *-ing* and *-ly* as still other chunks, then the burden on short-term memory would be limited to four thought units. Thus, the ability to identify multiletter chunks as a whole reduces the mental effort needed and speeds up the word identification process (Almasi, 2003). The reduced burden on short-term memory means that there is less of a disruption to comprehension as well. As noted in Chapter 2, third graders are developmentally at a point where this strategy is particularly important. Therefore, orthographic features should be a major component of your word identification instruction and assessment.

By using *context cues* as a strategy for identifying unknown word, the reader is able to use the context surrounding the unknown word to help identify it. Context cues enable a reader to form an expectation about the text (Ehri, 1991). These cues may come from the pictures, headings, subheadings, or text, enabling readers to make a guess, or narrow down the range of possibilities, that might make sense in a given context.

Assessing a student's ability to identify words while reading can be a difficult task, primarily because the strategies one uses to identify words is a covert, or hidden, process occurring in the mind. Thus, assessments must attempt to unlock the processes and strategies your students use while reading. Miscue analysis, word hunts, and word walls can accomplish this goal.

Miscue Analysis

You will be able to make some inferences about a reader's strategic processing by analyzing the miscues, or errors, made as they read aloud (Walker, 2000). Many teachers use informal reading inventories (IRIs) to analyze miscues. IRIs are commercially produced and consist of a series of reading passages, usually ranging in difficulty from emergent reading levels (preprimer) to eighth grade. Examples include the Basic Reading Inventory (Johns, 2005) and the Qualitative Reading Inventory (Leslie & Caldwell, 2006).

The purpose of an IRI is to assess through graded word lists and passages a student's oral reading, silent reading, and listening comprehension. These passages can be used to determine your students' independent, instructional, and frustrational reading levels, which alerts you to the types and levels of books they can read in a balanced literacy program. For example, books at a student's independent reading level can be used for independent reading activities such as Sustained Silent Reading (SSR) or Drop Everything and Read (DEAR). Books at a student's instructional reading level should be used for guided reading instruction. These books should offer some challenges for the student in word identification or comprehension, but they should not be so difficult as to frustrate the child. Therefore, with some instruction, the student will be able to read the book. Books at a student's frustration level are not recommended for guided instruction. These are books you might use as a read-aloud or recommend for parents or guardians read to the child at home.

IRIs can also be used to analyze the strategies your students use to identify words as they read which is most relevant for this chapter. Each commercially produced IRI has particular directions for administration; however, most IRIs follow similar procedures. First, students read word lists to determine at which level oral reading should begin. Then they are asked to read a passage at that level orally. During the oral reading the teacher records the student's miscues, or errors (see Figure 4.6 for one method of recording miscues). Following the reading, the student is asked to retell the passage and is asked several comprehension questions to determine comprehension level. Based on the student's performance on oral reading and comprehension, the teacher administers other passages of higher or lower levels to determine the student's independent (level at which the student can read fluently with good comprehension), instructional (level at which the student experiences a bit of stress while reading), and frustration reading levels (level at which the student is unsuccessful with decoding and comprehension).

If your main goal is to gain insight into the strategies your students use while reading, it is not important to use an IRI (Almasi, 2003). Any text not at the child's frustration level will suffice for that purpose because the goal is simply to determine the strategies used while reading. Thus, an alternative to an IRI is to have the student select a text that is neither too difficult nor too easy for him to read. This procedure is referred to as gathering a running record. For further information on gathering and interpreting running records, Peter Johnston's (1997) *Knowing Literacy: Constructive Literacy Assessment* provides excellent direction. As the student reads the selected text, you record her miscues, or errors. Many teachers can record the running record on a blank piece of paper. In fact, becoming proficient in taking a running record will make the process much easier. At first, you may find it easier to make a copy of the text on which to record the miscues.

After the text has been read and the miscues recorded, whether it is from an IRI or not, the next step is to analyze the miscues, which help reveal the cues and

Type of Miscue	Code	Example
Omission	Circle the omitted word.	Jill looked both ways (and) then began to cross.
Substitution	Draw a slash through the actual word and write the substitution above.	Jill looked both ways and then *begin* / be̶ga̶n to cross.
Mispronunciation	Draw a slash through the actual word and write the incorrect pronunciation.	She walked down our street to the *karmra* / co̶rn̶er.
Insertion	Draw a carat between the words in which the insertion was made and write the inserted word above.	She ⌃ *quickly* ran away.
Repetition	Draw arrows under the text that was repeated.	Jill saw the car and ran the rest of the way. ⟵—————————
Successful Correction	Draw a "c" with a circle around it to indicate that although there was a substitution initially, it was corrected.	Jill (©) *was* |sa̶w̶ the car and ran the rest of the way.
Attempted Correction	Draw an "ac" with a circle around it to indicate that although the reader attempted to correct the miscues he was unsuccessful.	The man in the car had to put on the| br̶akes. (ac) *balāk* *bakery*

FIGURE 4.6. Key for coding oral reading miscues when you have a copy of the text. From Almasi (2003, p. 36). Copyright 2003 by The Guilford Press. Reprinted by permission.

strategies a reader uses to construct meaning from text (Walker, 2000). Again, Johnston's (1997) book provides much greater depth, but a brief synopsis of interpretation is given here.

Some miscues are more significant than others (Almasi, 2003). For example, substituting *Dad* for *Father* is viewed as a nonsignificant error because it does not alter meaning. Sometimes a reader will make an error, realize it, and correct it. These miscues, known as self-corrections, are also not significant because they show that the reader was monitoring comprehension and using strategies to repair comprehension.

Uncorrected miscues and those that change meaning are considered significant. Those with the potential to affect meaning seriously include omissions, substitutions, mispronunciations, insertions, and repetitions.

Omissions occur when the reader omits a word, several words, parts of words, or a sentence. Omissions that change the meaning of the text are considered significant. Those that do not alter the meaning are not significant.

Substitutions tend to be the most frequently occurring miscues and occur when a real word is substituted for the word in the text (e.g., substituting *plot* for *pilot*). If the miscue alters meaning, it is considered significant. Readers who make numerous substitutions are attempting to bring meaning to the text; however, they may be overrelying on context cues as a strategy and not using letter-sound cues and orthographic features as word identification strategies.

Mispronunciations occur when a word is pronounced incorrectly. These miscues often result in a nonword (e.g., pronouncing *disaster* as *distra*) and are almost always significant because they change the meaning of the sentence. Readers who mispronounce words are usually using letter-sound cues as their word identification strategy (Almasi, 2003).

Insertions are infrequent but occur when the student inserts a word (or words) into the text. Usually these miscues are not significant if done in a limited manner. Good readers may insert a word here or there to make the text more fluent or more meaningful. However, if a reader inserts words consistently, this is a more serious problem in which the reader may be overrelying on background knowledge to read rather than attending to the print.

Repetitions occur when a word or phrase is repeated. Repetitions may enhance fluency and comprehension; however, they may also function as a delaying tactic in which the reader repeats a word or phrase just prior to reading an unknown word. When used as a delaying tactic, the reader is trying to buy time to decode the unknown word.

The type of information gained from a miscue analysis indicates the word identification strategies readers are using and whether they are monitoring their comprehension as they read. However, because miscue analysis is based largely on inferences, you may want to combine it with an informal chat with the students to see if they can explain their thoughts and strategies while reading. Goodman and Marek (1996) refer to this procedure as Retrospective Miscue Analysis (RMA). During RMA, the reader listens to a recorded version of the reading. Then the teacher and student discuss the miscues—whether they were semantically, syntactically, or phonetically similar to the actual text and how they affected comprehension. When miscues are semantically similar to the actual word, they did not alter the meaning of the sentence. When they are syntactically similar to the actual word, they may have been similar parts of speech and so fit into the sentence grammatically. Phonetically similar miscues are those in which the letters and sounds in the miscue are similar to those in the actual word. By reflecting on their reading in this manner, students can analyze and interpret the strategies they used to identify words and make sense of the text.

Word Hunts and Word Walls

Word hunts assess your students' abilities to identify and locate words in authentic texts that meet particular criteria. A lesson on teaching your third graders to identify chunkable words, for example, might point out that larger, polysyllabic words are good candidates for the chunking strategy, as well as why chunking is helpful in identifying unknown words. Thus, the lesson might focus on what chunking is, why it is helpful, and how to recognize chunks in larger words. The followup assessment might involve going on a word hunt. While reading a portion of their guided reading instruction text, students identify any words in which they could use chunking as a strategy. As they notice words in which they used chunking or could use chunking to decode the word, they record it on their Chunkable Word Hunt Recording Sheet (see Figure 4.7). It is important to allow time for students to discuss the words they record. During this discussion, students explain why each word they identified was suitable for the chunking strategy. The chunkable words, once discussed, can be placed in a column on a word wall.

Word walls are used to gather together words with similar features. In kindergarten and first-grade classrooms, word walls are often organized into columns of consonant sounds. However, in third-grade classrooms, the words might be organized to reflect the more mature word identification strategies third graders use. Thus, the headings might include chunkable words or words with particular prefixes, suffixes, or root words.

The open-ended nature of the word hunt, followed by discussion, is a way to assess whether students attained the objectives of your lesson without using a worksheet with particular right and wrong answers. Instead, students are challenged to read authentic text and to attempt to use the strategy. The recording sheet serves as a record of the types of words that might warrant the strategy's use. The discussion enables students to explain and provide the rationale behind their thinking.

ASSESSING COMPREHENSION/INTERPRETATION

The RAND Reading Study Group (RRSG) defined comprehension as "the process of simultaneously *extracting* and *constructing* meaning" (Snow & Sweet, 2003, p. 1). This definition highlights the important role that phonemic awareness, phonics, and word identification strategies play in text comprehension (*extraction*). However, it also recognizes that whereas print recognition is necessary, it is not sufficient to ensure comprehension. Constructing meaning is also a major component of successful comprehension. When readers construct meaning about text, they use and are influenced by (1) reader factors, (2) text factors, and (3) contextual factors.

Reader factors include those aspects that make readers unique (e.g., motivation, cognitive style, beliefs, and strategy knowledge) (Gaskins, 2003). Each reader

Chunkable Word (word and page number)	Is There a Prefix?	Is There a Root Word?	Is There a Suffix?	Cross-Check	
				Can I Pronounce It?	Does It Make Sense in the Sentence?
Example: playing	—	play	-ing	yes	yes

FIGURE 4.7. Chunkable word hunt recording sheet.

factor has an impact on how an individual responds to and interprets text (Beach & Hynds, 1991; Marshall, 2000). *Text factors* such as the type, length, readability, and content of the text will also affect the way a reader reads and understands (Beach & Hynds, 1991; Gaskins, 2003; Marshall, 2000). If the text lacks cohesion or is poorly organized, a reader may not be able to make sense of it. *Context* also plays an important role in determining how an individual comprehends text. For example, the instructional decisions a teacher makes in the classroom provide the context in which student readers find themselves (Beach & Hynds, 1991; Gaskins, 2003; Marshall, 2000).

Whether a text is read in school or out of school, alone or with a partner, silently or aloud, or with preparation or without preparation, each factor can alter the reading experience. Differences in any of these factors will affect the meaning readers construct. Thus, it is obvious that different readers, with different backgrounds and in different settings, may interpret a given text in different ways. However, we often expect all of our students to understand texts in the *same* way. That is, the tasks and assessments we use to determine whether students "comprehend" texts suggest that all readers should do so in the same manner.

As an example, I (JFA) discuss here an experience from my classroom. The year was 1986. As part of my teacher-guided reading instruction, one group of students in my class was reading an excerpt from the book *Sasha My Friend* by Barbara Corcoran. The children in this group were all fairly good readers in terms of their ability to decode and comprehend text. They did not excel as readers, but they did not struggle either. In the book, Hallie, a young girl who lives on a Christmas tree farm in Montana with her father, raises an abandoned wolf pup. She names the wolf Sasha. The two become close, although the wolf has to leave the safe environment in which Hallie nurtured her to live in the wild. About a year later, Hallie is walking through the forest when a lynx threatens her. From out of nowhere, Sasha leaps to wrestle the lynx to the ground and, in the process, saves Hallie.

After reading this excerpt, I encouraged the group to discuss it. At the time I was beginning to implement peer discussion into my classroom. That is, rather than asking comprehension questions, I was trying to encourage my students to generate questions and construct meanings about the text together. The questions they asked were not intended to be assessments of each others' comprehension; they were to be genuine questions that arose as they read the text. I had hoped to create an environment in which the group tried to help one another interpret and make sense of the text. One of the students wondered whether Sasha had attacked the lynx to save Hallie, the young girl who had raised her. At the time, my own interpretation was that this was the case. In fact, most of the children responded affirmatively to the student's comment, indicating that they, too, thought Sasha had intended to save Hallie. However, one boy in the group politely and respectfully disagreed. He stated something to the effect that, whereas this may be true, the text stated that during the attack Sasha looked at Hallie "as if she were a stranger." The student further noted that these words meant that the wolf had actually gone wild and could not have purposefully saved Hallie. Immediately, the group became highly animated and cognitively engaged. They were shocked and wanted to know where in the book it said that. They read and reread the text and, in a spirited but respectful manner, debated one another about the meaning of that event. As they discussed it, they realized they could not come to a conclusive interpretation. Some still believed that the wolf had saved Hallie deliberately; others agreed that the wolf must have gone wild and was merely looking for a meal when it attacked the lynx—saving Hallie was incidental. I myself was unsure. That's right—I was the teacher and I was unsure of the meaning of the text. The information this 9-year-old brought to the group was information I had never noticed or attended to before. The context of this reading (i.e., the peer discussion in which my students attempted to make sense of the text together) changed forever not only the way I think about and interpret the book, but also the way I think about reading and comprehension.

Previously, I had thought that "comprehension" meant that students should all understand the text in the same way. If I asked questions about it, there should be "right" answers. I did not consider that it might be ambiguous or that my students' backgrounds might lead them to different interpretations or that the context of the reading might influence them. I did not think readers could have multiple, and perhaps even conflicting, interpretations—until that day. As they read and reread the text (something they had never done previously), searching for evidence to inform their interpretation, they were more stimulated and cognitively engaged then I had ever seen them. I knew something magical was happening—my students were truly constructing meaning collaboratively. I didn't want it to end. They didn't want it to end. Afterward, some of the students begged to go to the library so they could check out copies of the entire book to determine if the author had left clues in previous or subsequent chapters. (They couldn't find any.) Others wanted to write a letter to the author in which they explained their interpretations and sought her perspective. (They did, but she never responded.) Students in other groups wanted to read the book to join in the fun. (I let them.) This one tiny literary experience ignited my entire class to read more, write more. In the end, they could not resolve the original issue, and it didn't matter. There was no "right" answer. There were multiple and conflicting interpretations, and it was wonderful. The students had truly engaged in a literary experience, and I wouldn't want it any other way.

I still don't care if there is a "right" answer. Sometimes textual issues have "answers" everyone might agree upon, and sometimes (most times) they do not. Environments with "answers" do not help children think divergently, critically, and evaluatively. Environments with "answers" do not encourage children to take risks because they fear they might be "wrong." Environments with "answers" tend to make children, especially struggling readers, passive and reticent. Our assessments of comprehension must, therefore, look beyond "right" answers to literal comprehension questions and attempt to assess the process by which children construct meaning.

The following are ways to assess students' abilities not only to *extract* meaning but also to *construct* it. Moreover, it is important to tap into multiple ways for children to express themselves. All too often we use only paper-and-pencil assessments to inform our instruction. Written assessments are just one means of assessing comprehension. Therefore, ideas for assessing comprehension through verbal, dramatic, and artistic responses are offered here.

Verbal Comprehension Assessments

Verbal assessments are one way in which children's comprehension can be evaluated in the classroom. Because talk evaporates very quickly, leaving no residue upon which to reflect, verbal assessments are not often used or valued in elementary classrooms. Yet, for some students the opportunity to express themselves verbally provides greater insight into their comprehension than any other method.

Vygotsky (1978) suggests that speech has an *organizing* function. Speech and language function as tools people use to think through concepts they may not have been able to piece together previously. That is, speech helps us organize and plan. Verbalization enhances our awareness by bringing subconscious (i.e., covert) thought processes to consciousness (Prawat, 1989). Thus, as we verbalize our thoughts and processes, our subconscious ideas become an object for reflection and evaluation. In terms of reading comprehension, when we give children the opportunity to verbalize their understanding, we are providing them with a forum in which their ideas about the text's meaning can coalesce. Their verbalization need not be polished or necessarily even unified. We simply need to provide space in our curriculum for our third graders to share their ideas (tenuous as those ideas may be) about text—about what makes sense to them and what does not. Three ways of assessing children's comprehension verbally are examined here: retelling, peer discussion, and think-alouds.

Retellings

Retellings require readers (or listeners) to verbalize what they remember about the text they read (or listened to) (Morrow, 1996). In effect, a retelling assesses the reader's ability to integrate textual information and reconstruct it. However, without experience in retelling many children find it difficult. Thus, Morrow suggests modeling, demonstrating, and engaging children in interactive retellings prior to them as an assessment. If the text is narrative, Morrow also suggests selecting texts with clear plot structures (definite settings, characters, several plot episodes, and a resolution). Texts with repetitive patterns (rhyme, repetitive phrases, and cumulative plot structure) lend themselves especially well to retelling. Once children are familiar with the retelling process, variations can be introduced, such as using story props (e.g., puppets, flannel board figures, stuffed animals, toys, and sound effects) to facilitate the retelling process and provide dramatic flair. Although many commercially prepared story props are available, children find it motivating to create their own.

Teaching children to use a retelling circle or story map also facilitates their oral retellings (see Figures 4.8 and 4.9). You might consider modeling how to add information to a retelling circle or a story map as you read aloud. After the read-aloud, model how to use the information you added to retell the story orally. Of course, you can also add story props during the retelling.

Retellings, when used as an assessment, primarily provide an indication of a child's literal recall of the text. In essence, retelling assesses the child's ability to *extract* details about the text, make inferences, identify cause–effect relationships, identify the sequence of events, and so on (Morrow, 1996). When done at regular time intervals, retellings can provide an indicator of students' growth over time. Morrow provides a detailed explanation of how to score retellings. First, divide the story into component parts: setting, theme, plot episodes, and resolution. Then identify the number of ideas in the text related to each part. It is sometimes helpful to create a template, or outline, of the story in which all of the main ideas related to the setting, theme, plot episodes, and resolution are grouped together and typed out. As the child retells the story, you can check off each idea in each category that is recalled. Thus, the assessment would indicate the proportion of total events in each category that the child is able to recall.

Retellings can also occur with informational text. You would have children retell the information, but rather than creating a template reflecting story structure, you would construct one reflecting the main ideas in the text (i.e., compare/contrast, description, problem/solution, sequence, and cause/effect).

Johnston (1997), however, reminds us that more proficient and less proficient readers retell text differently. In short, more proficient readers are better able to retell entire stories in sequence, whereas less proficient readers tend to provide abbreviated versions. Also, much of the less proficient reader's retelling must be drawn out of them by asking follow-up questions such as "Is there anything else?"

Johnston (1997) also reminds us that children from varying cultural and linguistic backgrounds will approach the retelling task in different ways. School teachers tend to be females with Anglo-European ancestry and middle-class backgrounds. The type of narrative structure with which they are most familiar presents stories in a linear, sequential fashion in which the setting and characters are described first, followed by an event-by-event recounting of the plot, and ending with the resolution. However, the narrative structure used in many Native American, Latino, and African American cultures has a cyclical rather than a linear pattern. When teachers expect a retelling to occur in a linear fashion and instead receive a "round about," cyclical retelling, they may score the retelling in a negative manner. This puts children from a cultural and linguistic background that is different from the teacher's at a disadvantage. Thus, we must be attentive to the cultural and linguistic backgrounds of our students.

Title: _____

Author: _____

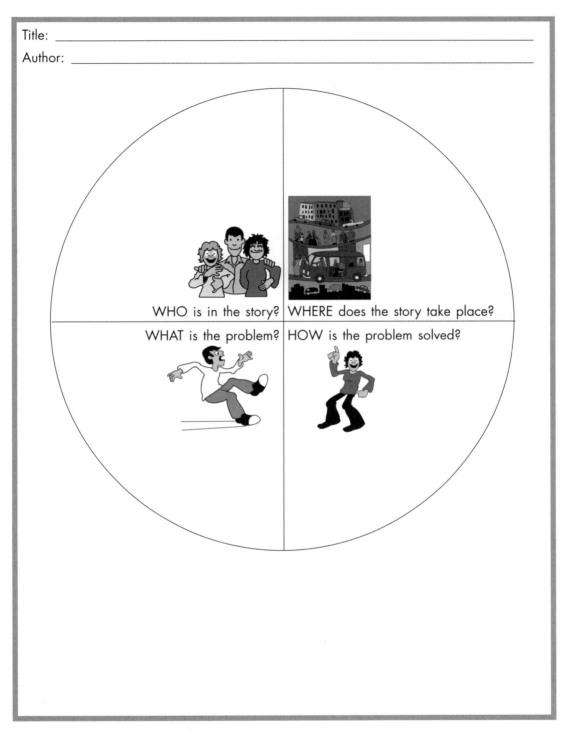

FIGURE 4.8. Retelling circle.

Title: _____

Author: _____

Setting	Characters	Problem or Goal	Attempts to Solve Problem or to Attain Goal	Solution
	Character Traits			

FIGURE 4.9. Story map.

Johnston (1997) also encourages teachers to make the retelling task as authentic as possible. Some students are resistant to retelling because it seems "phony." They think, "You read the story. I read the story. We both know what happened. Why do I need to tell you what happened?" Thus, Johnston suggests placing students in authentic situations in which retelling makes sense. For example, having a student retell a story to another student who did not read it makes sense, and the resulting retelling may be more genuine.

Overall, however, both Morrow (1996) and Johnston (1997) remind us that retelling does help students understand the manner in which texts are structured, which ultimately facilitates comprehension. Thus, using retelling as an assessment (while being mindful of requisite cautions) can be very informative for understanding your third graders' ability to recall text.

Peer Discussion

As mentioned earlier, peer discussion (see Gambrell & Almasi, 1996, for more information) is a different way of assessing comprehension. It provides a window into your students' abilities to *construct* meaning. The type of "discussion" occurring most frequently in elementary classrooms usually consists of a series of questions asked, or "initiated," by the teacher. After the teacher asks the question, he or she usually calls on students to "respond" to, or answer, the question. Following the response, the teacher usually "evaluates" the response by saying something like "yes," "good," or "well . . . not quite." The teacher might also use nonverbal communication such as a nod or a furrowed eyebrow to evaluate the response. These cycles of teacher question, student response, and teacher evaluation reflect an I–R–E (Initiate–Respond–Evaluate) structure, and they recur over and over again in typical classrooms (Cazden, 1986, 1988; Mehan, 1979). The cycles do not reflect discussion but are more of a quiz because the questions tend to be literal, factual, and closed-ended with predetermined or known answers. When there are predetermined questions with predetermined or known answers, discussion cannot truly occur (or be successful) because, if the answers are predetermined, there is little to really discuss. Likewise, only the student who supplies the "correct" answer actually participates. The other students are just waiting around until they are called on by the teacher. Thus, many students are cognitively disengaged, passive, or unresponsive (Dillon, 1985).

Peer discussion, on the other hand, is "a classroom event in which students collaboratively *construct* meaning or consider alternate interpretations of texts to arrive at new understandings" (Almasi, 2002, p. 420). Collaborative endeavors do not have predetermined directions or end products (Almasi, in press). Because the goal in peer discussion is constructing meaning, the end point is ever evolving and depends on participants' contributions. That is, what is discussed and where the discussion ends emerge throughout the peer discussion. Your third graders may enter the discussion with their own individual understanding, but that may change because in peer discussions students should be open to the ideas, opinions, and interpretations of others. Thus, their original interpretation may be shaped and transformed (Langer, 1992).

The teacher provides minimal assistance during these conversations. Instead, students determine the topics and negotiate the rules and social conventions by which they will conduct their discussion. That is, students determine the rules by which they will interact with one another (e.g., stick to the topic, take turns, respect others' ideas, and invite others to participate) and the direction in which meaning construction proceeds (e.g., making connections within the text, critiquing the author, and making connections to other texts).

The teacher's role is not to initiate topics of conversation, ask questions, or evaluate responses. Instead, to gain insight into students' comprehension, teachers need to listen to the discussion from the sidelines, taking anecdotal notes or memos of the strategies students use for interpreting text and for interacting.

The ensuing discourse can focus on personal reactions to, responses to, and interpretations of text. Almasi (2002) notes that students may also incorporate discussion of the strategic processes they use to make sense of the text. That is, they may display their ability to monitor their comprehension, make images (visualize), make predictions, or summarize the text. Students may also exhibit higher levels of abstract and critical thinking such as the ability to make connections between texts (intertextual connections), critique the author's craft, or evaluate characters' actions. The following example is from a recorded conversation of a group of third graders who had read a portion of Mary Pope Osborne's *Vacation under the Volcano* (1998), one of the books in the Magic Treehouse series. In this example, the children were making intertextual (text-to-text) connections. All students' names are pseudonyms.

> ALIYAH: In this book, Annie acts like this girl in the Bailey School Kids books. Her name is Liza, and she's always (*inaudible*).
>
> SIERRA: (*nodding her head affirmatively to Aliyah*) That was a good one.
>
> JOY: Yeah, well, it's usually [in the Magic Treehouse books] the boy [Jack] that's there, but this time she's there 'cause she's thinking all these things are weird [like] what's gonna happen next.
>
> SIERRA: This book reminds me of some like, um, this reminds me a lot of, um, that last book we had for our discussion.
>
> JOY: *Secret Fox?*
>
> SIERRA: (*Nods affirmatively.*)
>
> ALIYAH AND JOY: (*to Sierra*) How?
>
> SIERRA: Like . . . like the um, um the . . .
>
> PEYTON: *Secret Fox?*
>
> SIERRA: They had secret codes and stuff.
>
> PEYTON: I didn't have [read] that book.

SIERRA: 'Cause look, the first chapter is a secret code and he has a secret codebook.

JOY: Well, there wasn't a code. That was just a secret passageway.

In this example, the students use an interpretive strategy in which they make connections between the book they are reading and other books (intertextual connections). Aliyah believed one of the characters, Annie, acted similarly to a character in the Bailey School books. Joy noticed one of the characters, Annie, acting out of character when compared to her usual actions in the other Magic Treehouse books. These thoughts helped Sierra notice a thematic connection of secrecy between the current book and a book read previously. Later on in the same discussion, Joy thought the book reminded her of the movie *SpyKids 2*. The ability to recognize intertextual connections helps children think more broadly about the book. Instead of focusing simply on the literal details, these students were able to notice similarities in character actions and themes across texts (and movies).

As the teacher in this class, one way to assess would be to observe and take anecdotal notes. You might identify and record the types of interpretive strategies the students were using. To facilitate your note taking, you might consider using specification sheets (Matanzo, 1996) similar to those in Figure 4.10 to record the interpretive strategies and discussion behaviors exhibited by each student. Over time you could chart the types of interpretive strategies students use and how they use them. After analyzing this group's entire 20-minute discussion, we found that they used 12 different interpretive strategies (Almasi et al., 2004). The most frequent were using the text to verify points (19% of all talk), speculating or making predictions (15% of all talk), relating the text to personal experiences (14% of all talk), and examining the setting (12% of all talk).

You might also consider audiotaping or videotaping peer discussions throughout the year to include excerpts as evidence of comprehension growth. Viewing the discussion helps you see how the students construct meaning. For example, in their discussion of *Vacation under the Volcano* (Osborne, 1998), the group was perplexed by one of the characters, a woman (soothsayer) who issued warnings to the villagers of impending doom. Because this group had not yet read the entire book, students often made predictions, speculated about future events, and wondered about the motives of certain characters. This soothsayer was of particular interest because the students did not fully understand her motives or who she was. The group showed an interest in the character early in the discussion. However, the students repeatedly returned to that character as the discussion continued. It was almost as if they could not get her out of their minds.

PEYTON: All right, I wonder what the lady's name is. That lady's name that she like, she had a broken finger I think.

ALIYAH: The bony finger?

PEYTON: Yeah, the bony finger.

Evaluation Legend: Y = Yes; S = Sometimes; N = No		
Name:	Date:	
Text:		
Interpretive Strategies	**Self-Evaluation**	**Teacher**
1. Related own experience to topic		
2. Analyzed character actions		
3. Analyzed character motive		
4. Analyzed character interactions		
5. Critiqued author's style		
6.		
7.		
8.		
9.		
10.		
Discussion Behaviors	**Self-Evaluation**	**Teacher**
1. Initiated topics		
2. Responded to others		
3. Stayed on topic		
4. Avoided interruptions		
5.		
6.		
7.		
8.		

FIGURE 4.10. Specification sheet for use in assessments of comprehension during peer discussions. Adapted from Jane Matanzo (1996). Discussion: Assessing what was said and what was done. In Linda B. Gambrell and Janice F. Almasi (Eds.), *Lively discussions! Fostering engaged reading.* Copyright 1996 by the International Reading Association. Adapted by permission.

JOY: I'd hate, I'd hate to be like . . . like I'd hate to be her [Annie] showing me the warning. It would be like scary.

[Later]

PEYTON: I wonder what it would be like to live in that place [near a volcano].

JOY AND SIERRA: Ooooh!

JOY: And what if that lady, she was like always giving some warning, ya know, she just was scary.

In this excerpt the group identified the woman and expressed their fear. Later in the discussion, the students began to flip ahead to portions of the text they had not yet read and noticed a picture of the woman at a later point in the story. From what they had read thus far, they had envisioned an elderly woman; however, upon seeing the pictures, they began to reconsider.

PEYTON: I thought the woman would be old.

SIERRA: Me too, she sounds like she's old.

JOY: Yeah, I thought her hair would be like (*makes gestures like her hair would be all over the place*) ohohohoh (*points her finger*).

PEYTON: She's not old. She looks really nice.

SIERRA: Let me see.

JOY: Yeah, she looks nice in that picture.

SIERRA: What page is that?

JOY: Twenty-two.

PEYTON: Forty-three.

JOY: Forty-three? Well, maybe that's not the right lady. That's (*inaudible*). I think that's not her. I hope not. Well, it does say a woman. So, I don't know.

SIERRA: She's cute. She's not old.

PEYTON: She doesn't look old.

JOY: Yeah, see, look, she's smiling.

SIERRA: But if you see her hair, her hair (*inaudible*). She's not that old.

JOY: Yeah, 'cause I (*interrupted by Sierra*) . . .

SIERRA: Okay, then, right here it says she pulled out her library card (*reading from the book*). She has a secret library card.

PEYTON: I thought Annie pulled out her secret library card.

JOY: Annie did.

SIERRA: I think that's [the lady in the picture] the library, the owner of the library—master library—the library lady.

In this excerpt the students are attempting to understand the character better. The character issued warnings as if she knew something dire was about to occur. Through her words and actions, the students sensed that the character was elderly. However, as they encountered new evidence from the text, they began to question themselves and speculated about this woman's identity. Sierra went so far as to predict that the woman (soothsayer) was actually the master librarian who sends

Annie and Jack on all of their adventures from the Magic Treehouse. From this series of excerpts, you can see the group's cognitive wheels turning. The students are perplexed by the ideas before them, and they are engaged. In fact, during the discussion, Sierra noted, "I liked this book. It was so cool. First time I even read it I thought I was going to be bored, and then I got all the way into the book and it was cool. I liked it. I can't wait to finish it."

Peer discussion is a different way for children to make sense of the text. Rather than attempting to understand it on their own or through the teacher's questions, the group works collaboratively to build understanding. These powerful events can serve as a wonderful way to assess comprehension *as* it is being constructed.

Think-Alouds

Almasi (2003) described think-alouds as an assessment in which individuals express everything they are thinking as they perform a given task. Think-alouds go beyond traditional methods of assessing the products of reading comprehension (e.g., responses to comprehension questions, retellings, and summaries) to show how readers process text while they are reading (Kucan & Beck, 1997). Think-alouds enable you to see what strategies your third graders use as they read, when they employ them, where they employ them, and how they employ them. Thus you will learn when and where students use such strategies as those identified in Chapter 3 (see Figure 3.11), including tapping prior knowledge, making predictions, verifying/revising predictions, setting purposes, recognizing text structure, monitoring comprehension, and visualizing text.

Think-alouds are fairly simple to use. Unfortunately, they are rarely used in classroom instruction or assessment. Any text can be used for think-alouds, although it should probably not be at a child's frustration level so the cognitive demands are not excessive. Garner (1987, p. 69) suggests that think-alouds begin with general instructions such as "Tell me what you are thinking as you complete this task." Sometimes students may forget to reveal the strategies they are using; therefore, initial directions can be followed up with probes such as these: "Don't forget to tell me what you are thinking about" or "Can you tell me more?" (Wade, 1990, p. 444). As the student read the text aloud, they verbalize their thoughts, which can be recorded on video- or audiotape; you can also write them on a copy of the text. After the reading, you can record which strategies the students used, when they used them, and how well they seemed to work. You can also confer with the students, asking them to explain why they used a particular strategy and whether it was helpful.

Another way to use think-aloud as an assessment procedure, without having to listen to each student individually, is to encourage students to jot down the strategies they use on a sticky note. As students read, they place the sticky note at the point where the strategy was used. They might also draw a smiley face underneath the strategy to indicate whether it was successful or not. Afterward, you can have a postreading conference in which you chat about the strategies used, where they were used, why they were used, and whether they were helpful. Another method is to ask students to complete a chart on which they record the comprehension strategies they used while reading.

Think-alouds enable you to see how your students process text while they are actually engaged in reading, which will help you determine the effectiveness of your previous instruction and your plans for future lessons.

Written Comprehension Assessments

Written assessments of comprehension have traditionally consisted of responses to postreading questions (Pearson & Hamm, 2005), either multiple choice or open-ended. Unfortunately, many of the questions we ask students are literal and do not require readers to do much more than locate (or remember) facts from the text. Such assessments do not provide information that informs instruction. Instead, we should aim to create written assessments that, like peer discussion, engage students in the *process* of constructing meaning. Thus, students could engage in written assessments in which they work with a partner or a small group. Comprehension tasks and assignments should be open-ended to foster critical, evaluative, and divergent thinking. Where possible, they should also permit students to make choices. So, for example, after the peer discussion of *Vacation under the Volcano* (Osborne, 1998), a follow-up written assignment might be to work with a partner to think about ways in which the book was similar to and different from other texts students have read. This open-ended assignment requires students to think critically about all facets of the text (setting, characters, theme, and plot) in relation to other texts. You might suggest that they create a Venn diagram (see Figure 4.11), first to map out the ways in which the two texts are similar and different, and then as an outline for writing an essay in which they compare and contrast the two items. Students can also use other graphic organizers to make comparisons and contrasts. Figure 4.12 is a sample of a third grader's graphic organizer that compares and contrasts two characters.

Similar types of writing assignments might require students to describe a character's development throughout a book (a somewhat literal task) and then critically evaluate the choices and decisions the character made along the way. By adding the critical evaluation, you open up the task and learn how your students think about the character's choices and decisions. Any time children are thinking critically and evaluatively about the text it opens the door for thinking critically about the author. Written assignments critiquing the author's craft might include tasks in which your students consider whether they agree with the author, whether they think the author created believable or realistic characters, or why they believe the author included particular characters or events.

You might also consider having students write about their own emotions. For example, as students read each chapter they might chart their feelings with sticky notes along the way. Later they can examine their feelings and map them onto particular events in the text to see how their emotions changed with the plot. Students

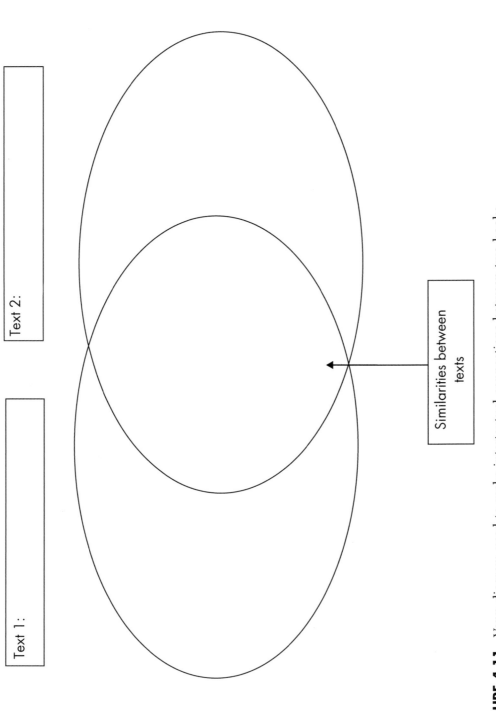

Text 2:

Text 1:

Similarities between texts

FIGURE 4.11. Venn diagram used to make intertextual connections between two books.

From *Teaching Literacy in Third Grade* by Janice F. Almasi, Keli Garas-York, and Leigh-Ann Hildreth. Copyright 2007 by The Guilford Press. Permission to photocopy this figure is granted to purchasers of this book for personal use only (see copyright page for details).

Third Grade—Compare–Contrast

Directions:

Today you are going to listen to a story called *Mufaro's Beautiful Daughters*. You will then write a response to a question about the story.

After listening to the story, complete the table below to help organize and plan your writing. Do not complete this table until after the story is read to you.

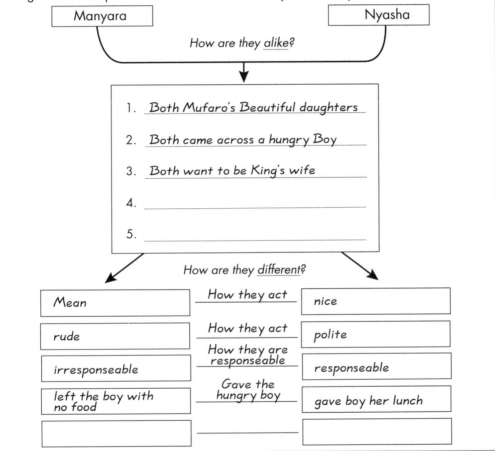

FIGURE 4.12. A third grader's comparison and contrast of two characters.

can work together with a partner to compare their emotions, write about how they changed over time, and explain what textual events caused those changes.

The key to better written assessments is to create open-ended tasks in which your students can work together. In this way, the assessment is not an end product with correct answers. Rather, it becomes an assessment of the way your students process and think about the text as they continue to make sense of it.

Dramatic Comprehension Assessments

Drama is yet another way for your students to demonstrate their understanding. Drama requires students to deeply understand the characters, setting, theme, and plot. Rather than simply describing these elements, students can breathe life into them. Plays and puppet shows are the most obvious and typical forms of drama used in the classroom. However, they might be more appropriately entitled "dramatic renditions." Unless the students truly reinterpret the characters and plot as a director might, plays and puppet shows really just reenact or reiterate the literal details of the text; that is, it is more of a retelling. To challenge your students to move beyond literal retellings, we must think of drama as a way to continue the meaning construction process.

One way to initiate such thinking is to recast the story in a different light. For example, after one of my (JFA) teacher-guided reading instruction groups read E. L. Konigsburg's *Jennifer, Hecate, MacBeth, William McKinley and Me Elizabeth* (1967), the students were interested in putting two of the characters on trial for witchcraft. In the book, two young girls, Jennifer and Elizabeth, are lonely and find themselves in need of friendship. Jennifer claims she is a "witch" and Elizabeth becomes her apprentice. The two communicate via secret codes and messages and establish a special bond as they conduct research in the library to find potions and ingredients to make a flying ointment. My students became intrigued with the notion of whether Jennifer was really a witch or whether she was pretending, to show Elizabeth she was different from other children. I usually tried to make time as we neared the end of a book for students to work together in some sort of self-planned, self-determined activity. In this case, the students were eager to create a trial in which those members of the group who believed Jennifer was truly a witch became the prosecution, and those members of the group who felt Jennifer was pretending became the defense. The groups worked for several days, gathering evidence from the text and researching in the library. They asked for a camcorder so they could re-create scenes from the text and enter it as "evidence" into the case, and they dedicated the entire literacy block (90 minutes) to reading, researching, writing, and acting. Most days, they also opted to stay in from recess to continue their work. They recruited another group in another class to serve as the jury, and they asked the teacher of another class to serve as the judge since they felt I might be biased. The groups chose members to act as characters from the book. These characters became their witnesses.

As each group prepared for the trial, the students wrote and rewrote the types of questions they would ask the witnesses and they considered how they might make rebuttals and closing arguments. The ensuing trial became an impressive (and humorous) display of the students' abilities to move beyond the text to make sense of the theme, the characters, their motives, and the author's intent. I did not need to see anything in writing for me to understand the process. I witnessed their construction of meaning as they worked eagerly and earnestly to build their case and as they dramatically pulled everything together in the courtroom. The key point here is that I did not "require" this task. From the beginning of the year, I simply made my literacy environment a place where children were encouraged to use any means possible to construct meaning. In the beginning I may have offered ideas, but as the year progressed the children generated their own ways of pulling the texts together. This trial is only one example.

After we had read a series of books featuring historical figures such as Ben Franklin, Beethoven, Johnny Appleseed, and Marie Curie, the group decided to have a panel discussion in which each group member became one of the historical characters. Other group members became journalists and talk-show hosts. The journalists were responsible for covering the event, and the talk-show hosts were responsible for preparing thought-provoking questions to elicit dialogue among the panelists. The idea was "what if all of these historical and folk figures could be in the same room at the same time?" What would they talk about? How would they respond to one another? How would they act? What would they wear? Each historical figure prepared by reading and rereading texts about their characters and how they might respond in such a setting. Meanwhile, the talk-show hosts and journalists prepared questions, as well as the stage. The students' preparation forced them to think beyond the texts to try to understand the historical and folk figures about whom they had previously read. As you might assume, the panel discussion itself was tremendous fun. The questions, responses, and ongoing dialogue were marvelous. The event did not require all students to be performers. Students who were shy or inhibited created roles for themselves in which they could participate comfortably. They volunteered to be the journalists, and rather than acting, they helped the talk-show host prepare questions and the historical figures prepare their costumes. Afterward, the journalists wrote newspaper articles about the event and published a mini-newspaper. When placed in these situations, students are highly motivated and eager to read, write, think, and perform.

Although these are just two ways to assess comprehension through drama, if you are able to create an environment in which your students know they are able to think creatively, they will generate their own ways to show their comprehension of text. But to go beyond typical plays and puppet shows, you might need to help your students think in a new way—a way that helps them move beyond the text to new understandings.

Artistic Comprehension Assessments

Like dramatic assessments of comprehension, artistic assessments should attempt to go beyond simple depictions of the story's characters, setting, and plot. Although such depictions (e.g., drawings, paintings, clay sculptures, dioramas, and mobiles) offer varied media, they still conform to the traditional expectation of assessing literal comprehension of narrative details. Instead, our artistic representations should go beyond textual details to encourage students to think critically. Also, artwork should somehow facilitate and exhibit the meaning construction process. Artistic endeavors should help students express their own opinions of, emotions about, and reactions to text.

Rather than reproductions of textual events, engage students in representations of their emotions. For example, color is often used by artists to symbolize emotions: Red often symbolizes anger; yellow, cowardice; gray and black, grief or despair. Crayons, colored pencils, paint, watercolors, chalk, and pastels, as well as various types of paper, can be made available in an art center. As your students experiment with color, they will create new ways to represent their emotional reactions to the text.

Texture can also be used to demonstrate emotion. Various textures—for example, silk, sandpaper, dried rubber cement, or a prickly pear cactus leaf—evoke different sensations and feelings: Silk is smooth and might represent calmness or quietness. Sandpaper might represent callousness, roughness, or gruffness. Dried rubber cement is tacky and sticky and might evoke being trapped or caught in a jam. A prickly pear cactus leaf, laden with spikes, might represent pain or agony. Students can use many different materials to represent their emotional reactions to text, thus encouraging them again to move beyond the text to interpret it.

Like color and texture, line can also be used to represent emotion. However, lines should not be used literally (e.g., drawing a teardrop to represent sorrow or sadness). Instead children can be encouraged to let the shape of a line reflect their emotions. Figure 4.13 provides two examples of how line might be used to represent varied responses to text. Think about what emotions the lines at the top of the page evoke. What might such an image say about a reaction to characters or an event? How do the lines on the bottom of the page contrast with the lines on the top? What emotions are suggested by the second set of lines?

When students use color, texture, or line to represent their feelings and emotions, they continue to interpret and bring meaning to text. As they become comfortable in expressing themselves in this manner, they may choose to combine color, texture, and line to create deeper, more complex representations of their textual interpretations. Artistic assessments of comprehension, when envisioned in a creative sense rather than as a means of representing literal details of the text, can become yet another way for children to express themselves and another way of assessing comprehension.

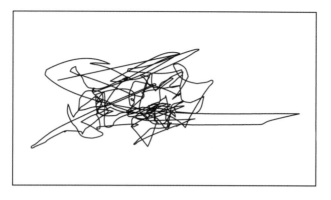

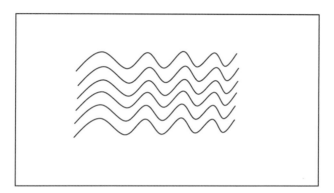

FIGURE 4.13. Artistic assessment of comprehension: use of line to represent emotional reactions to text.

ASSESSING VOCABULARY

Traditional vocabulary assessments tend to use a multiple-choice format. Beck, McKeown, and Kucan (2002) note that these assessments can provide an uncomplicated indication of word knowledge—if that is your goal. Moreover, performance on such assessments is highly correlated with a student's reading comprehension. However, Beck et al. also stress that word knowledge is not necessarily straightforward—it is complex and "falls along a continuum" (p. 96). That is, we "know" words on different levels and in at least four different ways. Some words we have never seen or heard. Other words we have heard but do not know the meaning of. Some words we are able to recognize, and we have a vague conception of their meaning. Finally, we know many words well and have a deep, conceptual understanding of them. To know a word goes beyond the simple definition that a multiple-choice assessment would indicate. Beck et al. remind us that word knowledge also includes the ability to apply and use a word in appropriate situations and recognize when it is used inappropriately. Knowing a word also involves understanding its multiple meanings and how they apply to other concepts. Thus, knowing a word's meaning is rather complicated, and as Beck et al. note, this complexity makes assessing word knowledge a difficult task. Students very often have a fairly good idea of the degree to which they know a word, so self-evaluations of word knowledge can be a fairly accurate assessment. A self-evaluation might consist of a list of target words and a chart (see Figure 4.14) on which children record the degree to which they feel they understand each word.

If your goal is to determine whether your student understands words fully and can use them appropriately, your assessments must be more complex than traditional multiple-choice tests. Beck et al. (2002) suggest several forms of classroom vocabulary assessments. First, they recommend simply asking students the meaning of particular words. Another assessment activity might require students to create examples (e.g., "Explain how someone acts if he is *sincere*," "Show what a person might look like if she were *horrified*"). Through extended explanation or performance, students are able to demonstrate understanding that goes beyond definition.

Beck et al. (2002) also recommend having students identify or differentiate between examples and nonexamples of words. If the word was *misconstrue*, you would present an example of it: "A journalist interpreted the information gathered from the interview incorrectly." And you would present a nonexample of *misconstrue*: "A journalist presented the information gathered from the interview accurately." Students have to determine which sentence represents an example of the word and which is the nonexample. In another type of assessment, students describe how pairs of words are alike and different (e.g., pretend/simulate; organize/categorize). This assessment indicates whether students can determine semantic similarity. Beck et al. also suggest having students place word phrases along a continuum, as in Figure 4.15, showing students how the meanings of different words compare. Students can also explain why they placed each phrase where they did, allowing further insights about each word.

Finally, Beck et al. (2002) recommend using a context interpretation task, in which students react to questions about sentences containing the vocabulary word. For example, if the vocabulary word was *chastise* and it was used in this sentence: "The teacher *chastised* the boy for reading books below his grade level," a follow-up question, such as "How do you think the teacher felt about the boy's reading ability?", would be asked to determine whether students could interpret the context of the situation in which the word was used. The ensuing explanation would help you understand whether students had a deep understanding of the word *chastise* and the contexts in which one might use it.

Each of these assessments is an informal way of understanding your third graders' word knowledge. They may take a bit of time to create, but with practice you will be able to use them as quickly as you would a traditional multiple-choice

Word	I do not know this word.	I have seen or heard this word, but do not know what it means.	I know this word a little bit.	I know this word well.

FIGURE 4.14. Student self-evaluation of vocabulary word knowledge.

Not excited at all ⟵――――――――――――――――――⟶ Very excited

How excited would you be if . . .

1. someone *agitated* you?
2. your dog *devoured* the chocolate cake you were planning to eat?
3. you *celebrated* your birthday in Disney World?
4. your baby brother *demolished* the project you had just finished?
5. you *prevailed* in the Olympics?

FIGURE 4.15. Placing word phrases on a continuum to assess vocabulary knowledge. Adapted from Beck, McKeown, and Kucan (2002). Copyright 2002 by The Guilford Press. Adapted by permission.

assessment. With these assessments, however, you gain a much more thorough picture of the degree and depth of understanding your students have about vocabulary words.

ASSESSING ATTITUDES TOWARD AND MOTIVATION FOR READING

Informal Observation and Assessment

One way to assess your students' attitudes toward reading is to carefully observe and take anecdotal notes of their behaviors as they participate in read-alouds, shared reading, teacher-guided reading instruction, and independent reading. This assessment will indicate whether students have a positive or negative attitude toward recreational reading and reading in academic contexts. Also, if you observe carefully, you will be able to discern how motivated students are during different literacy tasks. For example, you might consider rating each student's motivation on a 5-point scale (1 = highly motivated, 2 = motivated, 3 = indifferent, 4 = apathetic, and 5 = completely uninterested) periodically (perhaps once a week) during various literacy activities. Over time, you can develop a graph of the student's motivation for various activities, helping you understand the types of activities, texts, and contexts that affect motivation positively and negatively.

As students complete each activity, you might also consider having them evaluate their own attitudes and motivations for literacy by completing a self-evaluation form similar to that shown in Figure 4.16. As with your own data, you can teach students to graph and chart their level of motivation over time. This information can be used in teacher–student conferences to spark discussion about those activities, texts, and learning events that elicit higher and lower motivation.

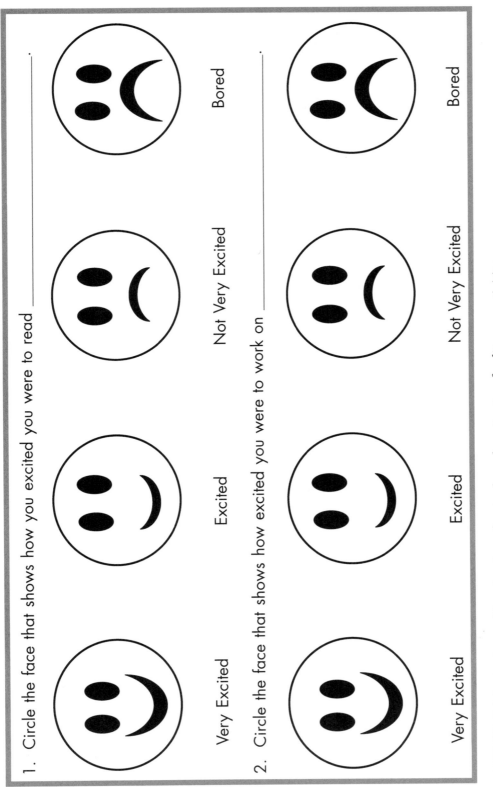

FIGURE 4.16. Student self-evaluation of attitude and motivation for literacy activities.

Formal Assessments

Informal teacher assessments and student self-evaluations have practical, everyday merit and can be incorporated into any literacy activity. However, there are also more formal assessments of students' attitudes that can be administered to your entire class at one time, usually within 15 minutes. Thus, it might be worthwhile to use a measure at the beginning of the year to gain insights about all your students' attitudes from the onset. This preliminary indication of which students may be more and less interested in reading will help you plan your instruction.

The Elementary Reading Attitude Survey (ERAS), developed by McKenna and Kear (1990), is a 20-item measure of children's attitudes toward reading, both recreational and academic. Sample items measuring attitude toward *recreational* reading include the following: "How do you feel about reading for fun at home?" and "How do you feel about getting a book for a present?" Sample items measuring attitude toward *academic* reading include these: "How do you feel when it's time for reading class?" and "How do you feel when the teacher asks you questions about what you read?" After each item, students have four response choices, each represented by the Garfield cartoon character: a very happy Garfield, a slightly happy Garfield, a slightly upset Garfield, and a very upset Garfield. The 4-point scale for each question means that a total raw score of 80 is possible (40 for the recreational reading subscale and 40 for the academic reading subscale). The entire measure is normed, so you can compare your students' scores to a national sample. For classroom use, however, it is more important to see which students have lower motivation than others so you can plan your instruction accordingly. The entire measure is available in *The Reading Teacher*, a journal published by the International Reading Association (see McKenna & Kear, 1990).

Another measure, Gambrell, Palmer, Codling, and Mazzoni's (1996) Motivation to Read Profile (MRP) is designed to assess a reader's self-concept and appreciation of reading. The MRP consists of a Reading Survey and a Conversational Interview. The Reading Survey is a 20-item multiple-choice questionnaire with a 4-point response scale. The 10 items related to self-concept are intended to provide information about students' perceived competence and performance in reading. Self-concept items include the following: "My friends think I am (a) a very good reader, (b) a good reader, (c) an OK reader, (d) a poor reader" and "I read (a) not as well as my friends, (b) about the same as my friends, (c) a little better than my friends, (d) a lot better than my friends." The other 10 items provide information about the value students place on various reading tasks: "I tell my friends about good books I read. (a) I never do this, (b) I almost never do this, (c) I do this some of the time, (d) I do this a lot" and "People who read a lot are (a) very interesting, (b) interesting, (c) not very interesting, (d) boring." The entire scale and directions for administering and scoring are available in an article from *The Reading Teacher* (see Gambrell, Palmer, Codling, & Mazzoni, 1996).

The MRP Conversational Interview is administered individually to students and consists of 14 open-ended questions designed to elicit information about motivation as it relates to reading narrative text, informational text, and general motivation for reading. The Conversational Interview provides information about students' motivation during authentic reading experiences and supplements the information gleaned from the Reading Survey. Gambrell et al. (1996) recommend individually administering the Conversational Interview to those students who exhibit low self-concept on the Reading Survey or are struggling readers. The authors also suggest that any information gleaned from the MRP be accompanied by close classroom observation to verify or reject any emerging hypotheses.

ASSESSING WRITING

Assessing students' writing, similar to assessing any other literary process, can be a formidable task. Traditionally, it is the end product of writing that is assessed. That is, the finished product is often the piece teachers grade and display for parents, administrators, and school visitors. It is important to discuss ways to assess the *products* of writing, but it is equally important to also assess the writing *process*. If we only assess final products, as we have mentioned throughout this chapter, we have little understanding of *how* our students write. It is only through ongoing assessment while students are engaged in the process of writing that we learn how effective our instruction has been and what is needed for our future growth.

Assessing the Process of Writing

Tompkins (2000) has noted the importance of moving beyond traditional assessments of finished products and examining what students do *as* they write. That is, assessments of the process of writing should attempt to uncover information about *how* your students write—the decisions they make, the strategies they use, and their thoughts throughout the process.

Portfolios provide a structure for process-oriented assessments. In general, portfolios are collections of student writing; however, to move beyond the "folder with a bunch of papers in it," we must include reflection. The portfolio, when used appropriately, should become a means for your students to learn about how they write and provide evidence of their growth (Tierney, Carter, & Desai, 1991; Tompkins, 2000). Students must give a high degree of thought to the pieces they select for their portfolios, which requires reflection on their own growth and development as writers. Each piece in a portfolio must be chosen carefully and included for particular reasons. Students should be encouraged to reflect on each piece of writing in terms of what they learned as they worked on it, how their writing has grown and changed while working on it, and how they hope to improve in future pieces (Tierney et al., 1991). Tompkins noted that many students find it difficult to write and think reflectively at first. Thus, we must model such thought processes as examples of the types of thoughts and words we use when we think and write reflectively about our work.

As with reading, careful observation and anecdotal note-taking are essential for assessing students' progress during process writing. Your observations might focus on how well students are able to gather and organize ideas during prewriting, how they approach drafting, how they function as they meet in small groups or with you to get feedback for revision, how they are able to use feedback to proof-read their own and others' compositions, and how they perform as they publish or present their writing (Tompkins, 2000). By jotting down notes from your observations throughout the writing process, you will be able to determine at what points some students struggle. This information can help you determine topics for future mini-lessons to help particular students. These mini-lessons can be designed for individual children or small groups who may all have difficulty with a particular strategy or skill.

Throughout the writing process, and particularly as students complete a piece, it is important to make time for children to reflect on their writing and their process. By simply writing a paragraph or a few sentences in which they reflect on what was easy (or difficult) as they wrote, students will be able to trace their growth over time. Students might also reflect on what they felt they did well, what strategies they used while writing, how (or whether) feedback provided during revision was helpful, what parts of the paper they were particularly proud of, and what they continue to need help with. Tompkins (2000) also recommended encouraging students to set goals for themselves for their next writing project. By reflecting on their most recent effort and setting goals for their next effort, students learn that writing is an ongoing learning process. Such reflection not only helps students chart and map their own growth over time but also provides feedback to help you plan future instruction. At various points throughout the year, students can glance back at their reflections to see how they struggled with some aspects of writing and how, with instruction, practice, and hard work, these same aspects became less difficult as the year progressed.

Assessing the Products of Writing

Usually written products are assessed by examining their quality. However, very often "quality" means different things to different individuals. Tompkins (2000) emphasizes the importance of identifying specific criteria for assessing writing from the onset. These criteria should focus on the goal of the writing assignment or task, rather than focusing solely on mechanics and grammar, as assessments often do. For example, if the goal of the writing assignment is to compare and contrast two texts, you should focus on how well students were able to compare and contrast. The goal of the assessment is to provide feedback for students so their ability to attain the *goal* improves. If we only provide feedback focused on grammar and mechanics, that is what students will work on to improve. Although grammar and mechanics will certainly improve general communicative ability and enhance clarity, focusing solely on these elements will not improve the *strategies* students use while writing (tapping prior knowledge, organizing ideas, visualizing, summarizing, making connections, revising, monitoring, etc.), their ability to attend to the *form* of the writing (e.g., story, essay, letter, poem, or journal entry), their ability to attend to the intended *audience* (e.g., oneself, classmates, teacher, parents, or businesses), the *text structure* they use to communicate (e.g., descriptive, narrative, persuasive, or expository), their ability to select and choose a *topic* for writing, or their ability to attend to the *purpose* for the writing (informing, entertaining, or persuading). Thus, the criteria you develop should focus on elements that will help students see how they can improve their writing.

In general there are two ways to assess and score written products: holistic and analytic (Moskal, 2000a). *Holistic scoring* involves gaining a general sense of the entire composition. Teachers begin holistic scoring by reading all the papers and sorting them into piles, ranging from strongest to weakest. The papers in each pile reflect similar overall strengths and weaknesses, and different scores or grades are assigned to each pile. Although teachers may consider content, specific criteria, and mechanics; none of these features is singled out or isolated. Instead, the score or grade is based on all features at once (Tompkins, 2000).

Analytic scoring differs from holistic scoring in that it allows you to evaluate the different components of a student's composition separately (Moskal, 2000a). In other words, analytic scoring permits analysis of specific traits or qualities in a composition (Tompkins, 2000), which will vary according to the task. Therefore, different tasks will each require the creation of different analytic scoring guides. Analytic scoring involves identifying the traits or criteria most essential to the task (Moskal, 2000b). For example, in a task in which students are comparing and contrasting two texts, important criteria might include the organization of text, content of ideas, style, and quality of written expression (mechanics and grammar). Once you have identified the criteria, you must determine the degree to which performance on each criterion will distinguish stronger papers from weaker ones. For the organization of text, for example, you would have to decide what in textual organization makes one paper better than another. Given that our sample task involves comparison, better papers might use cue words to signal comparison and contrast (*alike, similar, same, different,* and *unlike*). Also, better papers might present ideas in a logical order with clear topic sentences. So, the analytic scoring rubric should reflect not only the criteria but also how stronger and weaker writing differs on each one. Figure 4.17 illustrates how the criteria for organization of text might differ for stronger papers (scores of 4) and weaker papers (scores of 1). When developing descriptions to distinguish between stronger and weaker papers, Moskal (2000b) has recommended generating descriptions of the work rather than judgments. Rather than saying that the use of cue words was "excellent," identify a specific description, as in Figure 4.17: "Cue words are used frequently (more than

	1	2	3	4
Organization of Text				
1. Use of cue words	Cue words are not used at all.	Cue words are used, but rarely (once or twice).	Cue words are used regularly (3 or 4 times) and appropriately to indicate comparison.	Cue words are used frequently (more than 4 times) and are used appropriately to indicate comparison.
2. Presentation of ideas	Ideas are not presented in a logical order sentence by sentence or paragraph by paragraph.	Some ideas are presented in logical order, but order may break down midway through a sentence or paragraph.	Ideas are presented in a logical order either from sentence to sentence or from paragraph to paragraph but not both.	Ideas are presented in a highly logical and orderly manner from sentence to sentence and from paragraph to paragraph.
3. Use of topic sentences	Topic sentences are not used.	Topic sentences are used in one paragraph.	Topic sentences are used in at least two paragraphs.	Topic sentences are used regularly in all paragraphs.

FIGURE 4.17. Analytic scoring rubric for comparison writing task.

four times) and are used appropriately to indicate comparison." Use of such terms as "good," "poor," and "excellent," without specific description, is subjective from one person to the next. Thus, scores may have different interpretations for different scorers or from one moment to the next.

In developing analytic scoring rubrics, it is also essential to give your students a copy before they write their compositions. Then students can approach the task with a complete understanding of what is expected and how they will be assessed.

HOW DO I USE CLASSROOM ASSESSMENT TO FURTHER MY LITERACY GOALS AND MY LITERACY PROGRAM?

All of the assessments described throughout this chapter lend themselves to regular use in your third-grade classroom. However, in this section we will examine specific ways to use these assessments within the framework of a balanced literacy program, as outlined in Chapter 3. We will consider how you might use or recast the assessments during teacher read-alouds, teacher-guided reading instruction, shared reading, and independent reading.

How Do I Assess Growth during Teacher Read-Alouds?

Read-alouds are generally done with at least a small group of students and often with your entire class. Thus, you must consider ways in which you can assess multiple students while you are directly engaged in reading aloud. As a teacher, your ability to multitask is most likely very good; however, even the best teacher has difficulty in reading aloud, observing, and assessing 25 students simultaneously. Thus, you must consider ways of assessing that enable you to monitor several students at the same time. Every Pupil Response (EPR) techniques are one way to assess many students in a quick, efficient manner. Very often your objective during a read-aloud is simply to read for pleasure. When this is your objective, one very simple way to assess students' enjoyment while you are reading is to stop periodically and ask them to think about how much they are enjoying the text. Tell them that if they are really enjoying the text, they will give a thumbs-up sign. If they are really not enjoying it, they will give a thumbs-down sign, and if they feel lukewarm or indifferent, they will give a thumbs-sideways sign. Tell your students that they will not be responding until they hear the key phrase "Think, Ready, Respond." This phrase encourages students to think about their response to your question, to prepare, and then to respond. To try to preserve their privacy, you might ask students to close their eyes as they respond or look directly at you rather than at their peers. Because all students are responding simultaneously, your goal is not necessarily to record all the responses but to get a general sense of your class. When students are asked to think about their response to such a question, they will want to share their reactions. As much as you may want all students to participate, it is not always an efficient use of time. Thus, after students respond by using their thumbs, you might ask them to turn to a partner and briefly discuss why they feel as they do. This permits all students to voice their opinions in a manner that is less time consuming.

Another way to assess all students during a teacher read-aloud is to prepare EPR tags in advance. For example, if you were using your read-aloud as a way to model and think aloud about how to monitor your comprehension, you might prepare "stop" and "go" tags (a stop sign is reproduced on one side of the tag, and a go sign is reproduced on the other). As you read aloud, you might stop periodically to model or think aloud about whether the text makes sense or not. At other stopping points, you might ask students to stop and think about whether there are any confusing parts in the text that are making it hard for them to understand. At these stopping points, students would turn their EPR tags to "stop" if the text was not making sense to them and "go" if it was. As explained in Almasi (2003), it is helpful to have students explain the rationale behind their thinking because, while the text may make perfect sense to you or other students, it may not make sense to some students. Usually these students have very valid reasons for why the text did not make sense, which will help you plan future instruction.

How Do I Assess Growth during Teacher-Guided Reading Instruction?

Because the explicit instruction component of teacher-guided reading instruction consists of modeling, think-alouds, and demonstration of strategies and skills, usually the guided practice, or follow-up to that instruction, is when you would most often assess the progress of individual students, partners, or even small groups. Most of the assessments described in this chapter are useful during this phase of teacher-guided reading instruction. However, the nature of these assessments may change, depending on when you use them and whether they are intended to assess reading *processes* or *end products*. For example, if you taught your students how to monitor their comprehension in an explicit lesson and then modeled the monitoring of comprehension during a teacher read-aloud, you would want to assess during guided practice your students' abilities to monitor their comprehension.

Because comprehension monitoring is a *process*, occurring while one reads, you want to select a process-oriented comprehension assessment. To decide which assessments are most informative, consider the ideas in the comprehension section of this chapter. Retelling would not be appropriate because it assesses recall of textual details—an end product of comprehension. Peer discussion might indirectly assess students' ability to monitor comprehension, but because it usually occurs after reading it does not indicate whether students are using monitoring while they are reading. Because they are process-oriented, think-alouds (whether verbal, on sticky notes, or on a chart), in which your students note the strategies they use while they read, are the most informative means of assessing the ability to monitor comprehension.

If the objective for your lesson was more product-oriented, you would probably use an assessment of the end products of reading. The key is to be sure that the assessment actually provides information related to the objectives of your lesson.

How Do I Assess Growth during Shared Reading?

Shared reading, as a verbal activity in which more than one student is reading simultaneously, is difficult to assess. Because shared reading enhances fluency, it is difficult to assess fluency when multiple readers are reading at the same time. Using observation and anecdotal notes, you can capture the degree to which students appear to be participating but their growth in fluency. Thus, other than using observation, one of the best ways to assess growth during shared reading is to have students evaluate their own progress. As described in Chapter 3, you would encourage students to use a listening center to record their oral readings (after they have practiced on multiple occasions), play them back, and evaluate their fluency (see Figure 3.9).

How Do I Assess Growth during Independent Reading?

Because independent reading is linked to attitude toward and motivation for reading, some of the assessments described above (e.g., ERAS and MRP) will be helpful. However, you will be able to assess attitude and motivation during independent reading simply by observing and making anecdotal notes. Are the students (1) prepared (do they have a text selected in advance?), (2) engaged (are they actively reading?), and (3) motivated. You might also note the types of texts students are reading and consider (1) whether the texts are appropriate for their reading ability (not too challenging and not too easy), (2) whether the student is reading a variety of genres, and (3) whether the student is growing over time.

Students can also keep track of their own independent reading with a reading log, in which they note the titles, the authors, the genre, the start date, the end date, and a quick indication of their feelings about the text (see Figure 4.18).

Through observation, anecdotal notes, and student logs, you will begin to garner insights into your students' independent reading habits, which will provide evidence related to their attitudes toward and motivations for reading.

SUMMARY

Classroom assessment should give you insights into your students' literacy growth, and that assessment should enable you to be responsive to their needs. That is, your classroom assessments should tell you not only whether your students attained the objectives intended by your lessons but also the direction of future lessons. Classroom assessments should vary and can include conversational assessments such as metacognitive and text interviews. Observations and anecdotal notes can be used to assess nearly any literacy event. Miscue analysis is a way to assess the strategies students use to identify unknown words, and word hunts and word walls reveal whether students can recognize and identify words with particular features. Retelling, peer discussion, and think-alouds are verbal ways to assess the manner in which students make sense of text. Written, dramatic, and artistic assessments are also ways to assess student comprehension. Vocabulary assessment must focus on the degree to which students understand words. That is, assessments must move beyond simple definitions to determine deep understanding. Attitude and motivation for reading are also essential to literacy. Beyond observation and anecdotal notes, the ERAS and the MRP are more formal methods to easily measure students' attitudes and motivation at the beginning of the year. Portfolios are a process-oriented way to assess growth in writing, and holistic and analytic scoring can assess and score students' end products. Each of these tools can be easily implemented in a balanced literacy program consisting of teacher read-alouds, teacher-guided reading instruction, shared reading, and independent reading.

Name _____

Title of Text	Author	Type of Text	Date Started	Date Finished	Reaction

FIGURE 4.18. Student log for independent reading.

CHAPTER 5

A WEEK IN LEIGH-ANN HILDRETH'S THIRD-GRADE CLASSROOM

During my first year of teaching, the superintendent of the school district gave me a poster that read, "The object of teaching a child is to enable the child to get along without the teacher." That has been my motto ever since. The poster still hangs in my room. I have been teaching for 13 years. Most of that time I taught first grade, but for the last three years I have been teaching third grade.

Moving to third grade was quite a challenge. First, there was a whole new curriculum, second, a whole new kind of student. But did I have to change everything I had done in first grade? Not exactly. The most important thing I had done stayed the same in third grade, and that was teaching the students to be independent learners and to run the classroom. Yes indeed, my goal every year was to work myself right out of a job.

HOW DO I GET STARTED?

I spend the first month or so of the school year teaching students about routines and procedures. I want them to understand the importance of routines, but I also want them to learn to be flexible. So we start the year off with a daily schedule (see Figure 5.1). I post this schedule so students can internalize the routines.

Our Daily Schedule

8:10	Morning Routine/Meet 'n' Greet
8:30	Morning Broadcast
8:40	Spelling
9:00	Cursive Lesson
9:10	Read-Aloud and Snack
9:30	Specials
10:15	Math Lesson
11:15	Theme (Science, Social Studies, and Health)
12:00	Lunch
12:30	Writing
1:00	Guided Reading, Independent Reading and Response
2:00	Afternoon Wrap-Up
2:15	Dismissal

FIGURE 5.1. Sample third-grade daily schedule.

For instance, every day after specials we move into math. Students begin to enter the room, go to their desks, take out their math materials, and follow that day's math message (see Figure 5.2). They are already working before I even start the lesson. This is an example of students taking ownership of their learning.

The first time I see this, I call attention to it. "Ashleigh [all names used throughout this chapter are pseudonyms]," I say, "you are right on the ball, getting things done! Just like we talked about." I continue to praise the individuals who are taking ownership of their learning, and soon the rest of the students know what to do. I am grateful when they begin to internalize the schedule because it actually keeps me on task and on schedule.

Each day the students and I find ways to make the day run smoothly. For instance, one day Kayleigh said, "Mrs. Hildreth, every day when we get back from lunch, you put the lunch count tickets back in our slots. You know, I could do that." Another student adds, "Yeah, and every day you turn on the computers in the morning and you turn them off at the end of the day. I could do that." Suddenly, everyone in the class wants a job. So what do I do next? I pull out a job chart and create it with the students.

Math Message: Pretend you want to order carpeting to cover the whole classroom floor. How would you find out how many square yards of carpeting to buy? Be ready to talk about it.

FIGURE 5.2. Sample math message.

For many years I created job charts over the summer and put them up on the first day of school—and they never worked. Finally, I realized I was doing it all wrong. Now I wait until October to make a job chart, and I let the *students* make up the jobs. Inviting the students to be part of the process of running the classroom makes them feel important.

In the first month of school, I allot extra time for mini-lessons on routines, procedures, and responsibility. One very important lesson in the beginning of the year is the "What should I do when I am done with my work?" lesson. For some reason, in September the students' first response to finishing an assignment is to announce their "accomplishment" to the class and then to immediately ask, "What should I do now?" As part of the mini-lesson we create a poster for the room entitled "I'm Done! Now What?" (see Figure 5.3).

Other mini-lessons may include working with a partner, keeping your desk organized, making good choices, checking your work, and finding classroom materials and resources. Taking care of this business early in the year saves valuable time later. Also in the first month of school, I call on Fountas and Pinnell's (2001) *Guiding Readers and Writers* to map out the first 20 days of teaching reading. These 20 lessons help me establish routines and procedures for managing my reading workshop. I'll describe this more later in the chapter.

WHERE DOES THE DAILY SCHEDULE COME FROM?

At the beginning of each year, I sit down with my colleagues and we hammer out a schedule we can work with. We like to teach the same subjects at the same time because this helps with other scheduling issues that arise during the year. Our school district operates on a 6-hour day. Every day students get

- ➤ 30 minutes for lunch
- ➤ 45 minutes for special area instruction (physical education, art, music, or library)
- ➤ 60 minutes for math instruction

I'm Done! Now What?

• Check over your work.	• Finish another assignment.
• Read.	• Organize your desk.
• Free write.	• Do your job.
• Play a math game.	• Use the restroom.

FIGURE 5.3. "I'm Done! Now What?" chart.

> ➤ 45 minutes for science, social studies, and health (We alternate between teaching these three subjects, one unit at a time.)

> ➤ 20 minutes for routines like lunch count and attendance

> ➤ The rest of the day for literacy instruction, which includes whole-group reading, guided reading, read-alouds, independent reading, writing, spelling, and handwriting

As the year goes on, we tweak the schedule to meet the needs of the students and the curriculum. Of course, things always come up, like assemblies, fire drills, holiday celebrations, and so on, which means we often make adjustments.

HOW CAN I TURN MY KIDS ON TO READING?

Early in the year I spend a lot of time selling the kids on reading. One year, they actually booed when I first mentioned the word *reading*. I went home that night wondering how I was ever going to turn them on to reading. By the next day I had a plan.

That next morning I told them we were going on a family field trip. "Mrs. Hildreth, what is a family field trip?" they wondered excitedly. "You've never been on a family field trip?" I asked in astonishment. "Well, a family field trip is a field trip that you get to bring your family to. We will invite all of your families to meet at a local bookstore after school, and each of you will get to pick out a book to add to our classroom library. I spoke with our principal, Mrs. Laudisio, and she wants to come, too. She even said she would pay for all the books." The crowd roared with excitement.

I knew I would get a good response if I told the students that someone else was paying for their books. Of course, Mrs. Laudisio was not exactly paying for all the books, but she did give me permission to use my classroom budget money. I get about $300 a year, and I couldn't think of anything more worthwhile to put this money toward. It was an investment in our future.

Kids love field trips. I knew by engaging them in something they like (field trips) I would be enticing them to do something they might not like so much—yet (reading).

After this conversation, I sent a letter to the parents and invited them to join us. This turned out to be a great opportunity to talk with my students about their interests in books. Parents even offered to purchase books to add to the classroom library. This was also a great opportunity to discuss with parents the importance of reading and motivating young children to read. This was just the beginning of a year-long endeavor to instill a love of reading.

The next thing I did to foster reading was to read *Because of Winn Dixie* by Kate DiCamillo (1999) to the students. I knew they'd fall in love with this wonderful story of how a girl and a dog become friends. I had several copies of this book, and I noticed that by the third chapter all the copies were off the shelf. What's more, they were writing me letters about the book in their response journals. They were even talking about story characters over lunch.

One day during a class meeting, one of the students, Mark, said, "Mrs. Hildreth, you know Opal in *Because of Winn Dixie*? Well, I kinda know how she feels—not having any friends." "What do you mean, Mark?" I asked. "Well, lately I have been having trouble making friends," Mark admitted to us. This led the entire class into a lesson on friendship and making friends. Of course, this friendship lesson wasn't in my plans—who knew? But, nevertheless, theme time was thrown out the window and we discussed Mark's dilemma. That is why it is important to fill your room with lots of materials to foster literacy.

The third part of my plan was to have weekly conferences (explained later in this chapter) with students about the books that they were reading. I wanted to make sure they had the right books in their hands during independent reading and that they were getting the most bang for their buck. These reading conferences became a special time for us to chat, and the students never let me forget when it was their turn to be at the table with me. My goal is to develop attitudes and habits about literacy and learning that will last forever.

WHAT SHOULD I PUT IN MY CLASSROOM LIBRARY?

I know that many teachers receive very minimal funding for a classroom library. Another great way to stock a library without taking money from your own pocket is to use bonus points collected through book clubs. Each month I send a Scholastic book order home to the parents with an attached list of books I think are good picks. When parents purchase books, Scholastic gives our classroom bonus points that we can use toward the purchase of more books. I ask students to help me pick books they would like to add to the classroom library. I also order multiple copies (six) of books and use them for guided reading groups. Other bonus points are used to reward students with new books.

My classroom library is sorted by series, genre, and content. I used to have a section sorted by reading level until I asked myself, "What kid is going to come to the library with the intent of finding a good Level M book." My goal is to entice students with books. I want my classroom library to be inviting, not intimidating.

Similar to the IRIs discussed in Chapter 4, in my district we use the Developmental Reading Assessment (DRA), developed by Beaver (2001), to assess both fluency and comprehension. This information is meant to help teachers pick the appropriate level of books for guided reading lessons, as well as monitor individual reading growth from year to year. However, I don't draw attention to these levels, because I don't want my students to identify themselves as readers who are using levels. Reading isn't a race to reach a certain level. Reading is a useful tool. I want my students to identify themselves as readers—period.

I am continually adding new books to the library. But before shelving any book, I try to take it home and preview it first so I can sell it to the class: "Hey everybody, I have a new book to add to the library. I think you are going to love it. Especially you, Jona, because I know how much you like to read about football," I announce. (Now everyone is listening, and Jona is beaming with pride.) "This book is called *Tough to Tackle* by Matt Christopher [1971]." "Hey, I'm reading a Matt Christopher book," chimes in Brady, a reluctant reader in my class. "Well, then, I bet you would enjoy this book, too," I respond. Then I begin to tell the class how I took this book home and started to read it. I give a quick summary of what I read so far, and I ask whoever has a chance to finish this book to let me know how it ends. Then, of course, I ask Brady if he would add the book to our classroom library since he knows where to find the Matt Christopher books.

Sometimes keeping up with new books can be overwhelming, even though I have two young listeners at home. To alleviate the time crunch, I sometimes ask one of the students in my class to read the book at home. You can imagine how important the student feels when I ask for his or her help. When the student returns with the book, I ask him or her to give a brief book sell, and then we add it to the library.

If I am adding a new book to a series the children are already familiar with, I usually just say, "Hey, here's another great book about Jack and Annie. I wonder where the Magic Tree House will take them this time?" Most likely, the book is snagged out of my hands before I can even sell it.

HOW DO YOU SET UP THE PHYSICAL ENVIRONMENT?

As described in Chapter 3, each teacher should identify his or her overall goals for the classroom before setting up the physical environment. One of my goals is to help kids become independent, lifelong learners in a risk-free environment. I want them to enjoy learning and to be comfortable in our classroom community.

Our classroom has that "homey appearance" Taberski (2000) states in *On Solid Ground*. We have a large carpeted area with big pillows near the classroom library. I have curtains on the windows (don't tell the custodian, though), and we have some plants on the windowsill. Each student's chair has a cloth chair pack covering. The students' work is plastered everywhere.

We also have a round table, which is where I meet individually with students during one-on-one reading conferences, morning Meet 'n' Greet, and small-group guided reading instruction. In another area, students can check out theme materials and resources. There is also a computer section and a writing and art supplies section.

Materials are placed around the room so they are easily accessible to the children. Early in the year I do a "Where in the classroom can I find . . . ? (dictionary) lesson." I want students to seek out needed resources and materials and take responsibility for their own learning. The more I encourage this type of behavior, the more independent they will become.

WHAT DOES A WEEKLY SCHEDULE LOOK LIKE?

Each day we follow a similar schedule. It does not vary much from day to day. Monday's schedule is a bit different because I open with a Planning and Management meeting. Also on Monday the reading workshop looks different. Tuesday, Wednesday, and Thursday schedules are very similar. Then, on Friday, the reading workshop looks different again.

Although the daily schedules appear to be rigid, the key to good teaching is to be flexible. For example, sometimes I mesh two short weeks together. For instance, if a 2-day week is followed by a 3-day week, I plan those 2 weeks together as if they were 1 week. Sometimes, I will even use the short weeks to catch up and/or to review (remember all those lessons that went out the window?).

MONDAY SCHEDULE:

8:10	Morning Routine/Meet 'n' Greet
8:30	Morning Broadcast
8:40	**Planning and Management Meeting**
9:00	Spelling
9:15	Read-Aloud and Snack
9:30	Specials
10:15	Math Lesson
11:15	Theme (Science, Social Studies, and Health)
12:00	Lunch
12:30	Writing
1:00	**Whole-Group Reading and Target Skill Lesson** (Here I introduce a focus for the week through a whole-group reading. This sets the stage for Readers' Workshop on Tuesday, Wednesday, and Thursday.)
2:00	Afternoon Wrap-Up
2:15	Dismissal

TUESDAY, WEDNESDAY, AND THURSDAY SCHEDULE:

8:10	Morning Routine/Meet 'n' Greet
8:30	Morning Broadcast
8:40	Spelling
9:00	Cursive Lesson
9:10	Read-Aloud and Snack
9:30	Specials
10:15	Math Lesson
11:15	Theme (Science, Social Studies, and Health)
12:00	Lunch
12:30	Writing
1:00	**Readers' Workshop** (This consists of guided reading, independent reading, and response to text.)
2:00	Afternoon Wrap-Up
2:15	Dismissal

FRIDAY SCHEDULE:

8:10	Morning Routine/Meet 'n' Greet
8:30	Morning Broadcast
8:40	Spelling
9:00	Cursive Lesson
9:10	Read-Aloud and Snack
9:30	Specials
10:15	Math Lesson
11:15	Theme (Science, Social Studies, and Health)
12:00	Lunch
12:30	Writing
1:00	**Reading Conferences and Independent Reading** (I bring reading workshop to a close by engaging in one-on-one reading conferences in which the students and I meet individually to discuss the books that they are reading independently.)
1:30	**Book Talks**
2:00	Afternoon Wrap-Up
2:15	Dismissal

WHAT DOES A DAY IN A THIRD-GRADE CLASS LOOK LIKE?

If we look at each activity on the daily schedule in detail, here's what you'd see if you visited our classroom.

Morning Routine and Meet 'n' Greet

The students enter the room, and they know exactly what to do. First, they sign in and sign up for a lunch. Then they hang up their coats and sit down so they can read the front board and follow the directions in the morning message (see Figure 5.4).

While students are working, I ask each one to join me so I can do a Meet 'n' Greet. In the past, students used to wait in line after entering the classroom, but I hated the fact that they were just standing there. Now when they finish morning message, they come over to the table, bringing their assignment planner and home folder. We go through it together, and I check any notes/comments from home in the parent/teacher comment section in their assignment planner. I tell parents at open house that I will check their child's assignment planner every day and that this is the best place for them to communicate with me.

The purpose of a Meet 'n' Greet is twofold. First, it helps me with bookkeeping. Second, and most important, it gives me a chance to connect with the students socially. While looking through their folders, I have brief conversations with each child about . . . well, just about everything. If you know anything about 8-year-olds, you know they love to tell stories. This is one recent conversation I had with Lorenzo during our Meet 'n' Greet. "Mrs. Hildreth, guess what? My mom had a baby!" he announces. "Really?" I respond. "Yeah, and the baby has red hair just like me!" Lorenzo adds. "That's wonderful, Lorenzo. How about if I add that to our weekly newsletter?" "Sure!" he agrees.

The Meet 'n' Greet helps me to stay tuned in to what is happening in each student's personal and academic life and gives me the opportunity to make each child feel special each day. For example, after learning about Lorenzo's new sibling, I

Morning Message:

1. Did you sign in?
2. Make sure you have a good book for independent reading.
3. Complete math, page 67.
4. In your writer's notebook, brainstorm a list of at least three things you can do on your own. We will use your list during writing today.

FIGURE 5.4. Sample morning message.

realized the importance of such an event in his life and emphasized it by including it in the weekly newsletter.

Morning Broadcast

Every day our school has a morning broadcast, which is produced by the fourth and fifth graders. We participate in a patriotic song and the Pledge of Allegiance and then listen to important school announcements. At the end of every broadcast, the students say, "Make it a great day or not, the choice is yours." Our principal, Mrs. Laudisio, started saying this years ago, and now it has become our school motto. It is a great way to start each day.

Planning and Management Meeting

On Mondays I start the week by calling a Planning and Management meeting, which is held on the large carpeted area in the front of the room. I start the meeting by describing the week ahead. Students love to hear about upcoming events, but they also have a chance to tell any special stories or experiences. We usually end by discussing the issues from the previous week and then develop a plan for how to attack the issues that are still pending. Frequently, our talk involves social issues such as friendships, partnering, and just getting along.

Later in the week, I may feel the need to call another meeting. For example, last week I picked up my students from lunch, and immediately three of them were at my side, tattling on each other. I realized at that point that the tattling was getting out of control. I decided it was time for a team meeting. There goes writing—or maybe not.

At the team meeting, we discussed tattling. I began by saying that there is a difference between tattling and reporting. After a brief conversation about the difference, we filled in a compare/contrast graphic organizer. Then, with the little bit of writing time we had left, students created posters to remind us of all we'd learned in that day's unscheduled, but needed, meeting.

Spelling

As in many schools, our school has adopted a prescribed spelling program, which offers convenient spelling and language lessons. I begin the year by following the program solely because it helps with setting up routines and procedures. Later in the year, this spelling period evolves into mostly writing, with an emphasis on editing and revising. In other words, we use a company's program until the students realize spelling should be more connected to writing than to a particular subject called "spelling" that is scheduled at a particular time.

Read-Aloud

Read-aloud is my favorite part of the day. I always try to choose books I know the students will love. I want the class to connect with the book. I want to model good reading behaviors, such as how real readers think about text. For instance, while reading *The Doll People* by Ann Martin (2000), I stop when the dolls begin to come alive and say, "Can you imagine this? When I was a little girl I always pretended my dolls were real, but I don't think I ever imagined that they really came alive. I mean, think about it; you're fast asleep in your bed, and your dolls are having a good time in your room." Claire chimes in: "Yeah, and this reminds me of a movie I saw once—*Toy Story*. All the toys came alive."

I also use this time to demonstrate the comprehension skills and strategies I have been teaching during guided reading by encouraging students to discuss the text with me and each other. Later in the day, when I am targeting reading skills and strategies, I pull the read-aloud out and refer to it. For instance, if the target reading skill of the week is author's purpose, then we discuss the author's purpose of the read-aloud. This lesson facilitates a transfer of skills and strategies; I try to connect one literacy period to another.

At the beginning of the year, I use read-aloud time to introduce students to the books in the classroom library. My library consists of many series books, such as Junie B. Jones books, Katie Kazoo books, and Lemony Snicket's wonderful *A Series of Unfortunate Events* (1999). I pick one series a week to introduce. I read one of the books in the series, and depending on students' reading levels, I invite them to choose another one to read during independent reading time.

When choosing books, it is also a good idea to think about the science or social studies unit that is being taught. You can accomplish two goals at once. That is, you can integrate the same content into different subjects. Last year, while I was teaching a unit on immigration, I was also doing a Patricia Polacco author study. They fit together perfectly. In *The Keeping Quilt* Patricia Polacco writes about her grandparents' experiences while immigrating to America. This read-aloud may also carry over into writing since most of her books are memoirs, so this is a perfect time to study memoirs. I love it when everything fits together like a puzzle. Then, during writer's workshop, I may use Patricia Polacco's memoirs as a model for memoir writing. I would introduce the genre, model writing a memoir, and encourage students to try writing their own.

Math

My district adopted the Everyday Math program, which builds students' mathematical knowledge from the basics to higher-order thinking and critical problem solving.

I try to connect math to literacy as often as I can. For instance, before learning about measurement I always read *How Big Is a Foot?* by Rolf Myller (1962). This book activates students' prior knowledge about measurement and encourages them to make connections to the new learning that will take place in the next few math lessons. I also ask students to explain their mathematical thinking in writing. Most of the time when I ask them how they got an answer, they say, "I just knew it." Writing about mathematical thinking helps students think about their metacognitive processes.

Another way to connect math to literacy is through a vocabulary development strategy from Thoughtful Education (Silver, Strong, & Perini, 2001). This strategy—called a List, Sort, Label—is a variation of the List–Group–Label activity developed by Taba (1967). Students make a list of all the math words that they can recall from the previous unit. Then they work in groups to sort the words into categories. The students make up their own categories by grouping similar words together. Then they label each group. This activity encourages them to develop a deeper understanding of the previous unit's math vocabulary. While students are working on this activity, I circulate around to each group and assess the level of understanding. This activity can also be used as an anticipatory set before a unit's beginning to activate prior knowledge.

Theme

Theme includes science, social studies, and health, but our team focuses on one area at a time. The units of study are developed over the summer with colleagues and then taught throughout the year. Our team meets weekly to make changes to units, share ideas, and reflect on lessons we have taught. Often you can hear us bragging and/or bemoaning the lesson taught that day. The team collaboration helps us to constantly make the units better, so they are never the same from year to year.

Units of study are stretched across the curriculum. For instance, in third grade we study life cycles, which includes a close look at butterflies. While raising butterflies in our classroom we are continually reading and writing about them. During reading we focus on nonfiction text. We complete K-W-L charts (Ogle, 1986), compare/contrast graphic organizers, and practice making notes. This carries through into writing, when we compose compare/contrast essays and "how to" pieces (e.g., how to raise a butterfly). Similarly, our read-aloud consists of mostly nonfiction books about life cycles and butterflies.

Writing

Students in third grade write for many reasons and in all areas of the curriculum (e.g., I have shown how students use writing to explain their mathematical thinking and later I explain how students use writing to respond to their independent reading). Students also keep a learning log, in which they record thoughts about learning across the curriculum.

In my district, the students are required to write at least 10 pieces throughout the year, including personal narrative, compare/contrast essay, literary response, friendly letter, expository essay, poetry, persuasive essay, story, descriptive paragraph, and evaluative essay. Therefore, during writer's workshop, I introduce a required writing piece and teach its important components; then students write their own pieces, which are added to their writing portfolios.

Students also have an opportunity to write in their writer's notebooks, where they can write independently. They write, draw, doodle, record memories, list ideas, tell stories, record questions, and make drawings/sketches. These notebooks come in handy when students are searching for a topic to write about in one of the district-required writing pieces.

Every year I teach the students the Better Answer Formula developed by Cole (2002). This formula helps students write answers that look good and sound smart. It includes restating the question, developing a gist answer, providing details to support the answer, and ending with a concluding sentence. The formula also emphasizes staying on topic and editing strategies. The Better Answer Formula helps prepare students for the fourth-grade written response assessment given in our state.

Whole-Group Reading and Target Skill Lesson

Our district used to espouse literature-based instruction; that is, we had no corporate reading program. But recently, Scott Foresman was adopted. I use it for its skills sequence, although authentic children's literature is the heart of my program. The skills sequence is merely a way for me to be sure that I include necessary skills and strategies in my instruction and attend to my school district's policies.

On Mondays we start with a whole-group reading lesson and a target skill lesson, which sets the stage for the week. For example, if the target skill is *theme*, it is introduced on Monday and practiced throughout the week. That is, we discuss theme in our guided reading groups and independent reading conferences, and it even shows up in students' response letters. Again I try to help kids transfer learning from one situation to the next. I want them to know that skills and strategies are actually used beyond reading tests. Furthermore, these target skills and strategies are woven *everywhere* throughout the year.

Readers' Workshop

On Tuesdays, Wednesdays, and Thursdays, we engage in Readers' Workshop, in which three activities occur simultaneously: (1) the teacher meets with small groups of students for guided reading instruction, (2) other students work on independent reading, and (3) other students work on responding to what they have read.

If you enter our room during Readers' Workshop you might see that several things are happening at the same time. You would see me at a table, surrounded by five or six students and engaged in a guided reading lesson. You would probably hear me saying something like this: "Taylor, I'm so glad to hear you are clarifying while you are reading. That is what really good readers do!" or "Let's summarize what we read yesterday so we can make predictions for today's reading" or "What do you think is the theme of this book?" You might see students at another table writing a letter about the books they are reading during independent reading. I love to receive their letters every week, and the students can't wait for my response (see Figure 5.5). The letters help me learn about the students as readers. Some-

FIGURE 5.5. One third grader's Readers' Notebook entry and Leigh-Ann Hildreth's response.

times the students even ask me about the books I am reading. Depending on the guided reading lesson that day, students may also be working independently on short-answer response questions, filling out story maps, and/or making predictions for the next day's reading.

In another corner of the room you would most likely see students sitting knee to knee, eye to eye, discussing a text they are reading. This technique is explained in Cole's (2003) *Knee-to-Knee, Eye-to-Eye: Circling in on Comprehension*. This technique is taught to students at the beginning of the year. Or you may find students at various spots around the room, enjoying their favorite books. Most of the students like to cuddle up with the big pillows in the reading corner.

Setting up your classroom for Readers' Workshop is outlined in Fountas and Pinnell (2001) in the chapter "Getting Started: The First 20 Days of Independent Reading." Establishing routines and procedures for managing independent reading gets the Readers' Workshop off to a good start.

Guided Reading

As explained in Chapter 3, guided reading is a teaching approach designed to help individual students learn how to process a variety of increasingly challenging texts with understanding and fluency (Fountas & Pinnell, 2001). During guided reading, I meet with small homogeneous groups of children to enable them to expand their reading ability. I meet with each group approximately 3 to 4 days a week for about 20 minutes each day. In a class of approximately 20 students, I would most likely have three or four guided reading groups.

As explained in Chapters 1 and 2, by the third grade most students have good decoding strategies (except for struggling readers). They can read (or word call) just about anything put before them. Therefore, I mostly focus on comprehension. I model and teach strategies such as those outlined in Chapters 2 and 3: predicting, summarizing, identifying the main idea, making inferences, questioning, clarifying, and so on.

During guided reading, I introduce a book I have previously selected, based on students' reading needs. The selected book should provide a moderate amount of challenge, which I help students overcome.

What I do during guided reading:

> I introduce the text, and then students read independently.

> While the students are reading, I stop them periodically to make a teaching point. For instance, I might direct their attention to a portion of the text I did not understand at first.

> Then I will think aloud to show them how I clarified my thinking in that section of the text.

> I will then encourage students to continue reading the next section of the text and to be ready to talk about what they had to clarify while reading. It is important to tell students that really good readers clarify all the time.

> Before the students leave the table, I may give them an assignment to complete for the next day's lesson. For instance, I might ask them to read the next section of the text, fill in a graphic organizer, or even write a response to a question based on the reading they did that day.

For struggling readers, the guided reading session may look a bit different. These students may still need to learn some decoding strategies. Besides spending extra time on decoding strategies and word work, I also spend more time encouraging these students to clarify the text.

During Readers' Workshop, I encourage students to be "super silent" and to limit movement around the room. They are not allowed to use the bathroom unless it is an emergency. They are also not allowed to pick new books or interrupt me while I am at the guided reading table. I tell them that when they are not with me at the guided reading table, they have two choices: reading or writing about what they are reading—and that's it.

One-on-One Conferences

On Fridays I meet with students one at a time to discuss their independent reading books. I use this time with individual students to discuss book choices, check for understanding, reinforce reading strategies, and celebrate their reading. I use a checklist to assess their reading behaviors (see Figure 5.6). The items on this checklist were taken directly from the district report card. Besides using this information to guide instruction, I discuss it with parents at the end of each quarter.

Book Talks

Each week a few students are selected to do a book talk, or a book sell. At the beginning of the year, I demonstrate what this looks and sounds like and why we do it. Afterward, I invite all students to give at least one book talk. Later in the year, students sign up to give a book talk when they finish a good book. This is a great way for readers to practice public speaking, "sell" good books to other students, and most important, celebrate their reading successes.

SUMMARY

In summary, my goal is to encourage children to be readers and writers for real reasons: I want them to become independent, self-motivated learners. I want them to feel comfortable and loved in my classroom. I think structure and routines are important, but I also think there needs to be flexibility. I meet frequently with children individually and in groups. I let them know I value their thoughts and suggestions.

Each year I grow as a teacher. I learn from students, as well as from my colleagues. With every new class come new obstacles and new lessons. In this chapter, I have given you my favorite ideas. I encourage you to research new ideas, take risks, and most of all—learn from your students. Teaching children is one of the most rewarding experiences life can offer. Just the other day, a parent told me that for the first time her son is coming home happy and actually wants to talk about school. I was proud to be his teacher.

	Date:	Date:
_____'s Conference Record		
Text, genre, and level		
Automatically reads common and irregularly spelled grade-level words.		
Demonstrates appropriate rate, expression, and attention to punctuation when reading grade-level text aloud.		
Learns new words/vocabulary by examining its structure and placement in the text.		
Can accurately answer questions, using details from the story.		
Draws conclusions about events and characters.		
Summarizes main ideas from fiction and nonfiction text.		
Identifies and explains the underlying theme or message of a passage or story.		
Identifies relevant data, facts, and ideas in informational text.		
Creates/defends opinions, using information from the text.		
Interprets story elements such as characterization, plot, and setting to create meaning and understanding.		
Uses comprehension strategies to monitor and repair understanding.		
Monitors and self-corrects regularly to read text.		
Connects ideas in text to other ideas, experiences, and literature.		
E—Exceeds S—Secure	D—Developing	B—Beginning

FIGURE 5.6. Checklist for use during students' individual conferences.

CHAPTER 6

MEETING THE NEEDS OF INDIVIDUAL LITERACY LEARNERS IN THE THIRD GRADE

To enhance reading achievement, teachers must use what they already know about their students to carefully and creatively carve out a path for learning for each student in the classroom. Information gleaned from careful observation, interviews, surveys, assessments, and students' work, among other things, should be used to make decisions about how to meet the individual needs of students. These decisions are not always easy and may be altered frequently, based on updated information. In this chapter suggestions for how to begin planning for individual needs and how to meet individual needs daily, within a unit of study, and yearly will be outlined.

WHERE DO I BEGIN TO PLAN FOR INDIVIDUAL NEEDS?

At the beginning of each year, it is helpful to gain a perspective on your class as a whole in terms of the students' attitudes toward literacy, their motivations for reading, their instructional reading levels, the strategies they use to identify words, and their comprehension. Gaining an overview with initial data can help you plan general goals for your class, as well as for individual students.

As noted in Chapter 4, several assessments can be administered early in the year. McKenna and Kear's (1990) ERAS helps you to gain insight into students' attitudes toward recreational and academic reading. You can administer this scale to your entire class in about 15 minutes. Be sure, however, to read each item aloud

144

to your students rather than having them complete the measure on their own. This will ensure that all students, particularly those who may struggle with reading, can fully understand what is being asked. You want the score on the measure to be a true reflection of attitude toward reading, not reading ability.

The recreational reading subscale of the ERAS has 10 items, each weighted on a 4-point scale. When students circle the happiest Garfield cartoon character, they are given a score of 4, the slightly happy Garfield, a score of 3, the slightly unhappy Garfield, a score of 2, and the very unhappy Garfield, a score of 1. Thus, a score of 40 (10 items × 4 points) is the highest possible score, and a score of 10 (10 items × 1 point) is the lowest. Scores between 30 and 40 indicate students who really enjoy reading for fun, and scores between 10 and 20 indicate students who do not. The academic reading subscale of the ERAS is scored and interpreted similarly.

To illustrate how you might use such information to plan your instruction, we gathered authentic data from 20 third graders (who will remain anonymous) as part of a different research project (see Almasi et al., 2004). These data will be used to make up a "class" of third graders (see Figure 6.1). The first two columns of Figure 6.1 indicate scores on the recreational reading and academic reading subscale of the ERAS.

After entering the data, try to identify those students who seem to have particularly high or particularly low scores on each subscale. You might use two differently colored highlighters to indicate those students with particularly high or low scores. You might also want to total students' scores on both subscales to see who has the most positive and most negative attitudes toward reading. When coded in this manner, the data in Figure 6.1 reveal five students who seem to have the most negative attitudes toward reading of any type (students 1, 14, 17, 19, and 20). Their total scores were the lowest in the class (less than 50). Students 4, 5, 7, 9, 10, 11, 12, and 13, on the other hand, had fairly high scores on both subscales (greater than 60), suggesting that they have very positive attitudes toward any type of reading. With more students having relatively high scores, overall this class seems to have positive attitudes toward reading. So, in general you may not have to work on reading attitudes with the entire class, although you will need to worry about a few children. The ideas presented in earlier chapters will help you design environments to create more positive attitudes toward reading, to nurture those students who have negative attitudes, and to maintain the positive attitudes of the other students.

To gain insight into students' self-concepts as readers and the degree to which they value reading, you might administer Gambrell, Palmer, Codling, and Mazzoni's (1996) MRP. Like the ERAS, you can administer it in about 15 minutes, and because it is scored in a similar manner, interpretation is similar. If you have highlighted particularly high and low scores, you see that students 1, 2, 6, 8, 14, and 20 not only have low scores for self-concept as readers but also valued reading less. Combining this information with that gained from the ERAS, there is cause to worry especially about students 1, 14, and 20, who have negative attitudes toward

FIGURE 6.1. Sample data gathered in the fall of the year from a fictitious third-grade class.

Student	Gender	Elementary Reading Attitude Survey (ERAS)			Motivation to Read Profile (MRP)			Qualitative Reading Inventory (QRI)		Proportion of Each Type of Miscue Made at Instructional Level of QRI							Comprehension on QRI		
		Rec	Acad	Tot	Self-Conc	Value	Tot	Inst Level	Oral Acc	Self-Corr	Omit	Subs	Misp	Rep	Rev	Ins	Exp	Imp	Tot
1	M	27	23	50	26	24	50	3rd	94%	16	5	47	0	32	0	0	100	75	88
2	F	29	26	55	23	29	52	3rd	99%	33	0	17	8	33	8	0	100	50	75
3	M	32	27	59	30	35	65	3rd	97%	33	0	33	0	33	0	0	100	100	100
4	F	35	39	74	37	36	73	7th	98%	0	56	0	44	0	0	0	100	40	70
5	M	35	38	73	37	34	71	3rd	99%	0	0	50	0	50	0	0	100	75	88
6	M	27	31	58	25	28	53	3rd	95%	31	19	25	0	25	0	0	75	75	75
7	M	29	32	61	25	30	55	3rd	95%	41	6	29	6	18	0	0	75	100	88
8	M	32	23	55	28	26	54	3rd	97%	80	10	0	0	10	0	0	75	100	88
9	F	34	34	68	32	35	67	3rd	99%	100	0	0	0	0	0	0	75	75	75
10	F	36	31	67	34	38	72	3rd	98%	20	20	40	0	0	0	20	75	75	75
11	F	32	34	66	38	40	78	2nd	95%	20	7	13	0	53	0	7	75	75	75
12	F	35	31	66	24	31	55	3rd	92%	4	58	17	0	17	0	4	75	75	75
13	F	30	33	63	36	38	74	4th	90%	15	12	12	0	54	0	8	100	50	75
14	M	27	18	45	22	21	45	1st	84%	14	14	29	0	44	0	0	75	100	80
15	F	30	26	56	24	31	55	1st	88%	13	3	65	0	19	0	0	75	50	83
16	M	25	32	57	34	21	55	4th	93%	62	0	19	1	1	0	5	100	50	75
17	M	25	18	43	26	31	57	4th	96%	8	8	50	33	1	0	0	100	75	88
18	M	26	26	52	33	28	61	3rd	98%	17	33	50	0	0	0	0	75	100	88
19	F	25	14	39	32	33	65	1st	96%	14	0	29	57	0	0	0	100	0	50
20	F	23	18	41	25	28	53	2nd	97%	11	33	56	0	1	0	0	25	75	50
Avg		29.7	27.7	57.4	29.6	30.9	60.5		95%	26.6	14.2	29.1	7.5	19.6	0.4	2.2	83.8	67.0	78.1

Rec, Recreational Reading; Acad, Academic Reading; Tot, Total Score; Self-Conc, Self-Concept as a Reader; Value, Value of Reading; Inst Level, Highest Instructional Reading Level; Oral Acc, Oral Reading Accuracy; Self-Corr, Self-Corrections; Omit, Omissions; Subs, Substitutions; Misp, Mispronunciations; Rep, Repetitions; Rev, Reversals; Ins, Insertions; Exp, Proportion of Explicit Questions Correct; Imp, Proportion of Implicit Questions correct.

reading, have low self-concept as readers, and do not value reading. You might also want to also keep an eye on students 2, 8, and 17, as their scores on both measures are the next lowest in the class.

Students who have diminished self-concept as readers are especially worrisome because they are often less proficient readers. Therefore, those students with lower scores on the ERAS and the MRP might be the first students to whom you would want to administer an informal reading inventory such as the Qualitative Reading Inventory (QRI). As noted in Chapter 4, informal reading inventories indicate your students' independent, instructional, and frustrational reading levels. They also provide information about the types of word identification strategies children use and their comprehension. As indicated in Figure 6.1, students 14 and 20 have instructional levels below grade level. While working with them in teacher-guided reading instruction, the readability of the texts should be at a first-grade level for student 14 and a second-grade level for student 20. Texts above that level will prove frustrating for them. Because they both have a poor self-concept as readers (as indicated by scores on the MRP) and negative attitudes toward reading (as indicated by scores on the ERAS), you will not want to make reading a negative or frustrating experience.

The data in Figure 6.1 from the QRI also provide information about the proportion of miscues students made when reading at their instructional level (all children will make some miscues at this level). We determined what proportion of all miscues were self-corrections, omissions, substitutions, mispronunciations, repetitions, reversals, and insertions. These proportions are indicated in the columns with that heading in Figure 6.1. Notice that 56% of all of student 20's miscues were substitutions. This means that 56% of the time she was substituting one word for another, which would really hamper comprehension. You will note also that her comprehension scores (the last three columns of Figure 6.1) back up this hypothesis. These scores are the percentage of comprehension questions she answered correctly after reading the QRI text at her instructional level. In student 20's case, this was a second-grade text, in which she read 97% of the words accurately. However, 56% of her miscues were substitutions, and 33% of the miscues were words she omitted entirely. Yes, we would definitely expect her comprehension to suffer when making so many substitutions and omissions, and in fact, her comprehension was only 50%. Her comprehension of implicit information (e.g., inferential information) was higher, at 75% (see the last column of Figure 6.1), but her recall of explicit, or literal, information was only 25%. We see from all of the initial information gathered that student 20 is definitely a top priority. She is reading slightly below grade level, with poor comprehension, and has very negative attitudes toward reading. It is no wonder that she also has a low self-concept of herself as a reader.

Student 14, whom we were also worried about, is also reading below grade level, at first grade. His oral reading accuracy was 84%, which is particularly troubling because this score should be at least 90%. When we examine his miscues, we see that 44% were repetitions, which suggests that he is not reading fluently at even a first-grade level. Thus, there are two students who have particularly low attitudes toward reading, have low motivation, and are also reading below grade level. Student 1, who had low MRP scores and a fairly low ERAS score for academic reading, was reading on grade level, with good comprehension. So he may just be a student we need to motivate; however, we will want to keep a close eye on his reading throughout the year.

Once you administer the QRI to the students about whom you are most worried, you can gradually administer it to the other students in your class. In time, you will gain a more complete image of all students. It is important to gather such information, time consuming as it may be, for all students because, as you notice in Figure 6.1, there are two students (students 11 and 15) who had fairly positive attitudes toward reading and fairly positive motivation but were reading below grade level. If all the students had not taken the QRI, this information not have been known for awhile.

When examining all of the information in Figure 6.1, you will notice that four students are reading above grade level, five students are reading below grade level, and 11 students are starting the year with third grade as their instructional level—right where we would expect most students to begin. As discussed in Chapters 1 and 2, almost every third-grade class will have a range of reading abilities similar to that seen in Figure 6.1, which is why it is so important to provide differentiated instruction. If you used the same materials and the same methods to teach all the children, you would have at least five very frustrated and four very bored children in your class. The five frustrated children, over time, might begin to act out, or they may internalize their frustration, leading to low self-esteem and negative attitudes not only about reading but also about themselves. The four very bored children may also, over time, begin to act out because they are not being challenged enough. If you did not differentiate your instruction, nearly one-half of your class's needs would not be met.

With initial data such as those available to you in Figure 6.1, you will be able to make initial long-term plans for your entire class, form initial groups for teacher-guided reading instruction, and make plans for units and daily lessons. For example, you might make some initial guided reading groups based on instructional reading level, grouping the five students reading above grade level together, the four students reading below grade level together, and the 11 students on grade level together. However, as you work with these groups, you may see that they need to be mixed for particular lessons. The data in Figure 6.1 suggest that several students (students 4, 5, 12, and 17) rarely if ever self-correct their miscues, indicating that they have difficulty in monitoring their comprehension as they read—a critical reading strategy. Thus, you may want to group these students together (even though they have different instructional reading levels) to teach them how to monitor their comprehension. Of course, student 4 was reading at a seventh-grade level, so it is most likely that she *does* monitor her comprehension. She may not have self-corrected because she was reading so far above grade level. The other students, however, may need some instruction in that area.

In addition, unusually high proportions of the miscues of students 1, 2, 3, 5, 11, 13, and 14 were repetitions. When students make a lot of repetitions, it can be a sign of disfluency. That is, they may read in a halting, choppy, almost word-by-word manner. You may want to group these students together for guided reading instruction related to fluency (see Chapter 3 for ideas on shared reading). Students 4, 17, and 19 had a high proportion of miscues that were mispronunciations. For students 4 and 17, who were reading above grade level, this is not particularly worrisome, but for student 19, who is reading at a first-grade level, it is. A high proportion of mispronunciations, as indicated in Chapter 4, indicate that she may not be reading for meaning. When you note that her comprehension was also quite low, at 50%, you see the result of so many mispronunciations. Student 19 is also a worry, but for different reasons than student 20. Thus, the need for differentiated instruction is critical for *all* students—even those who seem to have a similar instructional reading level.

As you study the initial data, you should look for patterns, which will indicate many ways to group and regroup your students for guided reading instruction. Of course, as noted in Chapter 4, you will need to update and revise your initial plans according to the lessons you teach and the ongoing assessments you continue to make throughout the year. With the new informal data you gather every minute of every day, you will learn much more about your students, so you can make more stable hypotheses about the instruction they need. But data like those in Figure 6.1 at least give you an idea of where to begin.

Samples of initial long-term goals for this class might include (1) enhancing the attitudes toward and motivation for reading of all students, especially students 1, 14, 17, and 20; (2) challenging students 4, 13, 16, and 17, who are all reading above grade level; (3) enhancing the word identification strategies of students 11, 14, 15, 19, and 20, who are all reading below grade level; (4) enhancing comprehension strategies of students 19 and 20, who had low total comprehension scores; (5) enhancing the ability to make inferences from text of students 2, 4, 13, 14, 15, and 19, who all had low scores for implicit comprehension; (6) enhancing the ability to monitor comprehension of students 4, 5, 12, and 17, who appeared to have difficulty in self-correcting on the QRI; and (7) enhancing the fluency of students 1, 2, 3, 5, 11, 13, and 14, who had high proportions of repetitions on the QRI. Again, these are *initial* long-term goals. They are forwarded with caution because they are based on such limited information. As noted above, you will need to update constantly and revise your goals for each student, based on the information you gather daily as you work with your students.

HOW DO I PLAN FOR AND MEET INDIVIDUAL NEEDS DAILY?

There are a number of ways in which teachers can meet the needs of individual students on a daily basis. In this section, we will discuss the framework of differentiated instruction: "Differentiating instruction means changing the pace, level, or kind of instruction you provide in response to individual learners' needs, styles, or interests" (Heacox, 2002, p. 5). That is, differentiated instruction consists of respectful tasks, flexible grouping, and information obtained from ongoing assessment. Each of these ideas was discussed in Chapters 3 and 4; however, in this chapter, we provide snapshots of what differentiated instruction might look like when planning across different time intervals.

Teachers can choose to differentiate by content, process, or product, according to the students' readiness, interests, and learning profile (Tomlinson, 1999). When differentiating by content, you consider each student's individual interests in terms of subject matter. When differentiating by process, you consider each student's needs in terms of literacy processes (e.g., the word identification, comprehension, and writing strategies needed). When differentiating by product, you consider the ways in which individual students will best be able to show you what they have learned. That is, you will try to vary the types of tasks (e.g., written, verbal, artistic, and dramatic) and their format (e.g., small group, partner, individual, open-ended, and closed-ended) to meet individual students' needs. For example, let's say that according to your state's English Language Arts (ELA) curriculum, third graders should be able to "make, revise, and confirm predictions before and during the reading of a text." You would need to plan lessons to introduce and/or reinforce this strategy with the goal of its independent use in a variety of situations.

Based on your assessments, you may find that you have students who have a minimal understanding of what it means to make, revise, and confirm predictions and who read below grade level. You may also have students who have a basic understanding of what it means to make, revise, and confirm predictions but who need more guided practice in this strategy. You may have students who use the strategy and can work independently by practicing with new texts. By using flexible grouping and differentiating instruction by process—that is, the means by which the students come to understand and use the strategy of making, revising, and confirming predictions—it is possible to meet the individual needs of all learners.

For instance, your lowest group may need to step away from a written text and simply focus on the strategy of making predictions, say, in a lesson that has a cartoon as a text about which they make predictions. You can define making a prediction, explain and model how to make predictions, explain the importance of making predictions, and explain when to employ the strategy. Following your explanations, you would model for the students how to make predictions about what will happen next in the cartoon. You can stop the cartoon at various points to make, revise, and confirm predictions, which can be charted and discussed. In subsequent lessons, the strategy can be employed during the reading of texts at the learners' instructional levels and with continued modeling and guided practice.

Your middle group may simply need a short review of what it means to make, confirm, and revise predictions; how to do so; and when and why they are necessary. Then modeling, guided practice, and independent practice can be provided, using texts from the reading series or from guided reading.

Your advanced students can discuss as a small group what it means to make predictions, how to do so, and when and why they should be made. Then theme-related or other relevant books can be used for independent practice. For instance, you may, initially, want to place sticky notes in spots in the text where you would like students to make predictions. Eventually, students can put their predictions in the text on sticky notes for you to check. These predictions can become part of a peer discussion group.

In this example, you are teaching all of your students to make, revise, and confirm their predictions, but you are planning instruction to meet their individual needs and using materials at the appropriate instructional level.

As noted in Chapter 4, ongoing assessment of your students is the key to successful planning to meet their needs on a daily basis. Flexibility is also crucial. As shown by our sample data in Figure 6.1, just because a student is in the highest need group for instruction in one aspect of reading does not mean that he or she will be in the highest need group for all aspects of reading throughout the entire school year. Your teacher-guided reading instruction groups and small groups of children pulled for quick mini-lessons or extended practice will not and should not always be the same. Ongoing assessment should be your guide in forming readiness groups.

As noted in Chapter 3, students do not always have to be grouped by ability levels. Students can also be grouped by their interests. For example, children who are interested in a specific topic or genre, such as mystery, may wish to read a book and talk about it in a peer discussion group. All of the students do not have to be reading at the same exact level independently; books can be put on tape or buddy-read to help students for whom the book is too difficult to read independently.

Students' choices in forming groups and selecting texts are important for motivation and self-esteem. Students are very aware of groupings and text levels. In third grade, students reading on grade level are often reading chapter books. Those who may not be reading on grade level can be self-conscious about reading "baby" books or lower-level, less interesting, picture books. It is important to allow students to make choices from respectful tasks and texts. Student choice and flexible grouping are also important as you attempt to plan and meet individual needs within a unit of study.

HOW DO I PLAN FOR AND MEET INDIVIDUAL NEEDS WITHIN A UNIT OF STUDY?

Teachers will find through various assessments and observations that the academic, emotional, social, and affective characteristics vary from student to student and must be considered when planning units of study in literacy. A unit of study may focus on a specific text or sets of texts, which may be part of a reading series, trade books, or content area texts.

Again, student choice, ongoing assessment, and flexibility are extremely important. There are many ways to approach a unit of study while taking into account the needs of all learners. For example, after assessing students and taking into account their readiness, interests, and overall needs as learners, you can make decisions about what needs to be taught. Teachers should always refer to state and district curriculum guides and standards when making decisions about areas of instruction. It is also helpful to preview state assessments in order to determine what your students will be expected to do when taking these tests. The learners, the curriculum and standards, and the mandated assessments should be considered when planning units of study.

It is always helpful to bring together as many resources as the school has to meet the individual needs of learners. For instance, you can try to align your reading instruction time with other professionals in the building who are scheduled to work with your students, such as special education teachers, reading teachers, literacy specialists, and speech and language pathologists. You may also want to consider aligning your instruction times with other teachers at your grade level. Students in different classes can then receive reading instruction from various teachers that is based on their strengths and needs, thereby learning at their appropriate levels.

One way for the instruction of a unit of study to be organized is in stations or centers. One teacher or school professional would be responsible for teaching a particular area of the language arts. For instance, the literacy specialist may be responsible for word work. She may meet with a few students with the same needs once every 5 days. The lessons for each group would be tiered in order to instruct students at their particular levels. A classroom teacher may want to focus on writing. He would also meet with a small group of students once every 5 days or twice every 6 days. The number of days in the cycle and the number of times each teacher meets with each group would be determined by the teachers, based on the unit of study and the needs of the students. The reading teacher might focus on reading strategy instruction, and again students would rotate to her every couple of days.

This way of organizing instruction does not necessarily lend itself to a totally balanced literacy program, so you will need to be cautious when using it. It is likely that more reading instruction and practice would have to take place before or after these rotations during the school day. However, the rotating method of instruction does allow for students to be exposed to various teaching styles and to be a part of small groups whose needs are specifically targeted. This method can also cut down on management problems and alleviate some self-esteem issues for higher need students, who are usually the ones being pulled out for special instruction. For this model to be successful, all of the educators involved have to communicate and be responsible for anecdotal notes and assessments, so the classroom teachers of the students are kept informed on their progress. These groups can be changed on a monthly basis or whatever is agreed upon by the teachers and school professionals.

Another format that can be used to meet the needs of individual learners within a unit of study also calls on school professionals and grouping across grade-level teachers. Again, all of the groups can meet at the same agreed-upon time each day or on certain days of the week. The students would be grouped according to assessments, and the area of instruction would depend on the ELA curriculum, the students' needs, and the state reading assessments. Each teaching professional would take a homogeneous group of students and work on a particular skill or area of study, such as poetry, for a specified amount of time. These teachers would again be responsible for the assessment and evaluation of the students and for communicating these results to the classroom teachers. This format allows for a consistent teacher over time and a small-group setting in which students are given instruction that is based on their individual needs.

These are simply two of the many ways in which instruction can be organized to meet the individual needs of students within a unit of study. Teacher collaboration and flexible grouping are great ways to provide appropriate instruction. As a third-grade teacher, you must also consider what students have already learned in kindergarten and grades 1 and 2. You must also consider what students need to know to be successful in upcoming grade levels. These factors, as well as the factors of your learners and curriculum, must be taken into account as you plan to meet the individual needs of your students over a school year.

HOW DO I PLAN FOR AND MEET INDIVIDUAL NEEDS OVER A YEAR?

When I (KG-Y) first began teaching third grade in New York State, the education department was just introducing sets of standards for each subject area. We were asked to gear our instruction to meet these standards, as well as to district curriculum and pacing guides and a reading series scope and sequence. There was a state test in reading at the third-grade level and some district assessments at the end of the school year.

With the No Child Left Behind (NCLB) Act now so prominent, states are held even more accountable for the progress of their students. States have to adopt assessments in ELA across grade levels, and an increasing number of states are adopting core curriculum and standards with performance indicators for ELA (many of these can be found online). Of course, as noted at the beginning of this chapter, we cannot forget students' strengths, needs, and interests in our planning and instruction.

When I first began teaching, we attempted to pull together all of the state and district requirements to maximize our instructional time and help foster connections for students by developing thematic units. The curricular planning consisted of a series of webs, or maps, drawn from the lists of standards and district requirements across subject areas. These maps were helpful because they included activities and texts and allowed us to pool best practices and resources. They did not, however, take into account what the students had learned prior to third grade or what they would learn in subsequent grades. The maps were often used by the people who created them, but they were not necessarily used by other teachers in the district or viewed by other grade levels. Moreover, the creation of these thematic units was very time consuming.

Now many districts are turning to curriculum mapping. Jacobs (1997) discusses the benefits of teachers using the calendar, as well as technology, to record ahead of time or document after instruction the content and skills to be taught and implemented or those that were already taught and implemented. These maps are then read by grade-level colleagues in the building and are edited for gaps, repetitions, alignment with standards, and so on. Next the maps are read by people outside the discipline or grade level. Everyone looks for ways to make the maps better. Then a large group or the entire faculty reviews all of the feedback from the smaller sessions, and revisions are made. For instance, if two different grade levels are using the same text, it is determined at what grade level that text will be used in the future. This helps to fill in gaps for students and alleviate repetition of texts and units of study.

Curriculum mapping is just one way to meet the individual needs of learners over a school year. When implemented at a districtwide level, such long-term planning can be used to meet these needs for the students' entire school career in the district. Regardless of the method used, careful planning with constant evaluation and revision are crucial.

SUMMARY

Chapter 6 provided suggestions for beginning to plan for and meet the needs of individual students on a daily basis, within a unit of study, and over the school year through instruction differentiated by content, process, or product. Ongoing assessment and flexible grouping, as well as allowing students' choices, are all important in meeting the individual needs of learners on a daily basis.

Creatively using time and resources can lead to varied instructional groups for different units of study. Make the most of the professionals with whom you work and pay close attention to frequent assessments to guide your instruction and make decisions about grouping students. Finally, use a system of mapping to plan your school year. Share the maps with colleagues to avoid overlap and gaps, and be open and flexible to revisions.

CHAPTER 7

RESOURCES

(L-AH) remember the day I stepped into my first classroom. I remember it vividly because it was the scariest day of my life. What now? Where do I start? Materials? Resources? Lessons? I was lost. Five years of college, preparing me for the job I'd wanted since I was a child, had left me with no idea of where to begin. Even after years of experience, my colleagues and I continue to find new answers to our favorite literacy questions. Let me share some of them with you.

HOW DO I FIND GOOD BOOKS FOR THIRD GRADERS?

The only way to find good books for third graders is to ask them to discuss the books they have chosen to read. Once a week, try starting your literacy block by asking the students to tell the class why they picked the book they are reading and to give a brief summary of it. This is a good way to learn about their reading interests.

During a recent reading conference, one of my students said, "Mrs. Hildreth, I just finished *The Bad Beginning* by Lemony Snicket and I loved it! Did you know that the author actually warns you not to read this book because there are so many unfortunate events? I think he really wants kids to read it. Are there any more books like it?" Once I realized he was so interested in Lemony Snicket, I ordered the rest of the books in the series. His excitement over the *A Series of Unfortunate Events* books sparked interest throughout the class. This is just one example of students taking the lead, but the truth is that this kind of thing happens all the time in my class.

Marvin Redpost books by Louis Sachar
Jigsaw Jones mysteries by James Preller
Magic Tree House books by Mary Pope Osborne
Katie Kazoo books by Nancy Krulik
Cam Jansen books by David Adler
The Boxcar Children books by Gertrude Chandler Warner
Capital Mysteries by Ron Roy
My Weird School series by Dan Gutman
Stanley books by Jeff Brown

FIGURE 7.1. Books to stock in your classroom library.

Reading is contagious. Other students will start choosing certain books to read because they heard their fellow classmates talking about it. You could also ask students to give book talks to recommend books to other students in the class.

Third graders enjoy a variety of texts, especially humorous books like *Calvin and Hobbs* comic strips by Bill Watterson, adventure texts like *The Magic Tree House* series by Mary Pope Osborne, realistic fiction like the Cam Jansen series by David A. Adler, and older books like E. B. White's *Charlotte's Web*. Other students love to read nonfiction, especially texts that ooze facts about sharks and other sea creatures.

Every month I send in a Scholastic book order, always ordering new books with the bonus points. Purchasing books through Scholastic, Troll Carnival, or Highlights for Children book clubs is a great way to stock your library. These clubs offer the most recent books, as well as many classics at reasonable prices.

Every month the students look forward to the books being added to the classroom library. Sometimes they even tell me what books to get. When the new books come in, I call the students over to the rug, introduce the new books, and tell them why they were ordered. I can tell right away which books they will love. Figure 7.1 shows books to include in your third-grade classroom library.

I try to buy multiple copies for guided reading or class sets for whole-group reading. The titles in Figure 7.2 spark peer discussion. I also gather books for teacher read-alouds (see Figure 7.3).

Coerr, E. (1977). *Sadako and the thousand paper cranes.* New York: Penguin.
Creech, S. (2000). *The wanderer.* New York: HarperCollins.
DiCamillo, K. (2000). *Because of Winn Dixie.* Cambridge, MA: Candlewick Press.
Lemony Snicket's *A Series of Unfortunate Events.* New York: Scholastic.
Lowry, L. (2002). *Gooney bird Greene.* New York: Houghton Mifflin.
Martin, A. (2000). *The doll people.* New York: Hyperion.
Martin, A. (2003). *The meanest doll in the world.* New York: Hyperion.

FIGURE 7.2. Great books for peer discussion.

Bridges, S. Y. (2002). *Ruby's wish*. San Francisco: Chronicle Books.
Cannon, J. (1993). *Stellaluna*. Orlando, FL: Harcourt, Brace.
Demi. (1997). *One grain of rice: A mathematical folktale*. New York: Scholastic.
Ernst, L. C. (1998). *Stella Louella's runaway book*. New York: Simon & Schuster.
Greene, R. G. (2004). *This is the teacher*. New York: Dutton Children's Books.
LaMarche, J. (2000). *The raft*. New York: HarperChildrens.
LaMarche, J. (2003). *The elves and the shoemaker*. San Francisco: Chronicle Books.
London, J. (2003). *Giving thanks*. Cambridge, MA: Candlewick Press.
Munson, D. (2003). *Enemy pie*. San Francisco: Chronicle Books.
Scieszka, J. (2004). *Science verse*. New York: Viking Juvenile.
Scieszka, J. (1995). *Math curse*. New York: Viking Juvenile.
Stevens, J. (1995). *Tops and bottoms*. Orlando, FL: Harcourt, Brace.

FIGURE 7.3. Books third graders love to listen to.

Each year, add books to your library. Use classroom budget money or bonus points from book clubs, write grants, or ask for donations from parents. Other good sources are yard sales, bargain bookstores, and local libraries. Don't forget to purchase books to go along with your science and social studies curricula. Invite the students to help you choose books for the classroom.

HOW DO I FIND INSTRUCTIONAL ACTIVITIES TO INCLUDE IN MY LITERACY PROGRAM?

Over the years I have found many ways to locate instructional activities.

Surround Yourself with Resources

The books in Figure 7.4 suggest many instructional activities. Use sticky notes to mark the ideas you want to try. There are also many books to consider when you are looking for ideas related specifically to reading and assessing reading (see Figure 7.5). I also consult several texts on writing (see Figure 7.6).

Cunningham, P. M., & Allington, R. (1999). *Classrooms that work: They can all read and write*. New York: Longman.
Harwayne, S. (2000). *Lifetime guarantees: Toward ambitious literacy teaching*. Portsmouth, NH: Heinemann.
Routman, R. (1991). *Invitations: Changing as teachers and learners K–12*. Portsmouth, NH: Heinemann.

FIGURE 7.4. Great resources for literacy activities.

Almasi, J. F. (2003). *Teaching strategic processes in reading.* New York: Guilford Press.

Bear, D. R., Invernizzi, M., Templeton, S., & Johnston, F. (2004). *Words their way: Word study for phonics, vocabulary, and spelling instruction* (3rd ed.). Upper Saddle River, NJ: Pearson.

Beck, I. L., McKeown, M. G., & Kucan, L. (2002). *Bringing words to life: Robust vocabulary instruction.* New York: Guilford Press.

Clay, M. (1991). *Becoming literate: The construction of inner control.* Portsmouth, NH: Heinemann.

Cole, A. D. (1998). *Literacy activities for building classroom communities.* Scarborough, ON: Pippin.

Cole, A. D. (2002). *Better answers: Written performance that looks good and sounds smart.* Portland ME: Stenhouse.

Cole, A. D. (2003). *Knee to knee, eye to eye: Circling in on comprehension.* Portsmouth, NH: Heinemann.

Cole, A. D. (2004). *When reading begins: The teacher's role in decoding, comprehension, and fluency.* Portsmouth, NH: Heinemann.

Fountas, I. C., & Pinnell, G. S. (1996). *Guided reading: Good first teaching for all children.* Portsmouth, NH: Heinemann.

Fountas, I. C., & Pinnell, G. S. (1999). *Matching books to readers: Using leveled books in guided reading, K–3.* Portsmouth, NH: Heinemann.

Fountas, I. C., & Pinnell, G. S. (2001). *Guiding readers and writers grades 3–6: Teaching comprehension, genre, and content literacy.* Portsmouth, NH: Heinemann.

Fountas, I. C., & Pinnell, G. S. (2002). *Leveled books for readers grades 3–6: A companion volume to guiding readers and writers.* Portsmouth, NH: Heinemann.

Fox, B. J. (2000). *Word identification strategies: Phonics from a new perspective* (2nd ed.). Upper Saddle River, NJ: Merrill.

Gambrell, L. B., & Almasi, J. F. (1996). *Lively discussions: Fostering engaged reading.* Newark, DE: International Reading Association.

Gunning, T. G. (2001). *Building words: A resource manual for teaching word analysis and spelling strategies.* Boston: Allyn & Bacon.

Harvey, S., & Goudvis, A. (2000). *Strategies that work.* Portland, ME: Stenhouse.

Invernizzi, M., Johnston, F., & Bear, D. R. (2004). *Word sorts for within word pattern spellers.* Upper Saddle River, NJ: Pearson.

Johnston, F., Bear, D. R., Invernizzi, M., & Templeton, S. (2004). *Word sorts for letter name–alphabetic spellers.* Upper Saddle River, NJ: Pearson.

Morrow, L. M. (2002). *The literacy center: Contexts for reading and writing* (2nd ed.). Portland, ME: Stenhouse.

Oczkus, L. D. (2003). *Reciprocal teaching at work: Strategies for improving reading comprehension.* Newark, DE: International Reading Association.

Opitz, M. F., & Rasinski, T. V. (1998). *Good-bye round robin: 25 effective oral reading strategies.* Portsmouth, NH: Heinemann.

Raphael, T., Pardon, L, Highfield, K., & McMahon, S. (1997). *Book club: A literature-based curriculum.* Littleton, MA: Small Planet Communications.

Taberski, S. (2000). *On solid ground: Strategies for teaching reading K–3.* Portsmouth, NH: Heinemann.

Tierney, R. J., & Readence, J. E (2000). *Reading strategies and practices.* Upper Saddle River, NJ: Pearson.

(continued)

FIGURE 7.5. Great resources for reading activities.

Tompkins, G. E., & McGee, L. M. (1993). *Teaching reading with literature: Case studies to action plans.* New York: Merrill.
Trelease, J. (1979). *The read-aloud handbook.* New York: Penguin.

Resources for Reading Assessment

Johnston, P. H. (1997). *Knowing literacy: Constructive literacy assessment.* Portland, ME: Stenhouse.
Moore, R. A., & Gilles, C. (2005). *Reading conversations: Retrospective miscue f analysis with struggling readers, grades 4–12.* Portsmouth, NH: Stenhouse.
Paris, S. G., & Stahl, S. A. (2005). *Children's reading comprehension and assessment.* Mahwah, NJ: Erlbaum.
Tierney, R. J., Carter, M. A, & Desai, L. E. (1991). *Portfolio assessment in the reading–writing classroom.* Norwood, MA: Christopher-Gordon.

FIGURE 7.5. (*continued*)

Use Technology as a Resource

When starting a new unit or a new book, try using a search engine like Google to find information about it. Also, many teacher-oriented websites are very useful. Some charge a small stipend, but others are free. These websites offer ideas, reproducibles, and other important information to help make daily lesson planning easier. Bookmark teachers' websites such as www.enchantedlearning.com, www.proteacher.com and any others you find.

Join Local, State, and National Reading Councils

Reading councils plan annual conferences, which produce very good teaching ideas, and some plan brunches and author events and engage in community outreach. For example, all of us (JFA, KG-Y, and L-AH) are members of IRA; our state affiliates, the New York State Reading Association (NYSRA) and the Kentucky Reading Association (KRA); and our local IRA affiliate, the Niagara Frontier Reading Council (NFRC). The last is actually one of the ways in which we got to know

Calkins, L. M. (1986). *The art of teaching writing.* Portsmouth, NH: Heinemann.
Fletcher, R, & Portalupi, J. (1998). *Craft lessons: Teaching writing K–8.* Portland, ME: Stenhouse.
Fletcher, R., & Portalupi, J. (2001). *Nonfiction craft lessons: Teaching information writing K–8.* Portland, ME: Stenhouse.
Harvey, S. (1998). *Nonfiction matters.* Portland, ME: Stenhouse.
Tompkins, G. E. (2000). *Teaching writing: Balancing process and product* (3rd ed.). Upper Saddle River, NJ: Merrill.

FIGURE 7.6. Great resources for teaching writing.

each other better—we are all past presidents of our local council. Some local and state councils offer literacy grants, which can help you purchase materials for your classroom.

Attend Local Conferences and Workshops

Conferences and workshops can be sources for teaching tools, ideas, and techniques. Many presenters are good at sending off attendees with usable ideas for immediate use in the classroom. Recently, I attended a conference sponsored by my local reading council. The guest speaker was Cathy Collins Block, who spoke about buddy reading. When I returned to school on Monday morning, I explained the new method of buddy reading I had learned at the conference, and the students couldn't wait to try it. I continued to use this strategy for the rest of the year. My students even taught it to other third graders in our school. After my students internalized the strategy, I assigned it for homework: teaching the strategy to their parents. Figure 7.7 shows the homework assignment sheet I sent home with my students.

Survey Your School's Multiple Copy Sets

Some schools have book rooms to house multiple copies of leveled books. If you are fortunate enough to have this resource, it is wise to be familiar with the available titles. If this resource is not available, it makes sense to start your own library. Again, you might pay for multiple copies with classroom budget money or bonus points earned through book clubs such as Scholastic. You could also work with other teachers at your grade level, and pooling your money and books would eliminate duplicate sets.

Subscribe to Literacy Magazines and Journals

Literacy magazines and journals such as *The Reading Teacher* (published by the International Reading Association) and *Language Arts* (published by the National Council of Teachers of English) are a great resource for new teaching ideas based on current research. *The Reading Teacher* is published eight times a year, and *Language Arts* is published six times a year—providing teaching ideas all year long.

Survey Anthology Manuals

Many schools adopt literacy programs that provide teachers' manuals, a resource for teaching skills.

Use Colleagues as a Resource

The best ideas are often only a few steps away. Find out what resources and ideas your colleagues have, and let them know what you have to offer. Share lesson ideas and brainstorm other methods. For example, while writing this chapter I thought

April 22, 2005

Dear Parents:

This week our class has been practicing a new activity in reading. We call it *Buddy Read with Me*. Students work in pairs. In this activity the students are practicing many important third-grade strategies such as oral reading, summarizing, questioning, and predicting. We use this activity with nonfiction text.

As part of tonight's homework, please ask your child to demonstrate this strategy for you. You will need to be your child's partner. Your child should be able to tell you what to do.

As part of our third-grade Life Cycles theme, we are studying butterflies and moths. We will actually be raising butterflies right in our classroom. Please use the *Buddy Read with Me* activity to read pages 18–35. After using the activity to read the text, please fill out the survey below. Thank you for your help with this project.

Sincerely,

Leigh-Ann Hildreth

Name: _____

1. How well do you think your child knows this strategy?

2. Was your child able to summarize the text, including the main idea? What did you notice?

3. Does your child seem to enjoy using this strategy?

4. Do you think you will use this strategy at home when you are reading nonfiction text with your child?

FIGURE 7.7. Sample homework assignment sheet sent home to parents.

it would be a good idea to survey my colleagues on what books they use for literacy lessons and how they use them. One colleague, Mikal Brennan, keeps a stack of very good read-alouds in a big basket in her room. At the beginning of the year, she reads most of them to her students for enjoyment. She also talks about story elements such as setting, characters, problems, and solution. While she is reading, she demonstrates how "reading is thinking" by verbalizing her thoughts about the story, thereby setting the tone for her Readers' Workshop. She often models making connections, wondering, predicting, and previewing text. These read-alouds are then put into the basket.

Later in the year, Mikal uses these same stories to teach literacy lessons. For example, at the beginning of the year, she reads *When Jesse Came Across the Sea* by A. Hest. Later, she uses the same book to model visualization, introductions, and happy endings. When the familiar book is reread, the students are able to focus on the author's craft rather than on the content of the story. She may continue to use this book throughout the year to remind the students what really good readers and writers do.

Mikal starts many of her literacy lessons by reading excerpts from these books. She continues to add books to this basket throughout the year. She also uses the same books year to year, adding and deleting books to meet the needs of her students. I imagine that using the same books over and over helps her to know what each book offers.

Mikal's passion for these special books was evident as she picked up each one to show me. She oohed and ahhed over every book in the basket, and I bet her students do the same thing. Quite often they choose these stories during independent reading time.

I realized that I already own many of the books Mikal has in her basket (see Figure 7.8). All I need now is a basket. She was even kind enough to put sticky notes on each book to remind me what it will help me to teach. So, sometimes the best ideas are right next door.

SUMMARY

There are many ways to find resources for your classroom. Children's literature is essential for creating a rich, literate environment. Although books can be expensive, you can purchase them by using book club points, writing small grants, and searching libraries. Professional resources are also important for keeping up-to-date with current research and practice. Purchasing books, using technology, attending conferences, subscribing to journals, examining basal anthologies, and chatting with colleagues are all ways to broaden your repertoire of teaching ideas.

Making Connections:

Bunting, E. (1994). *Smokey night*. Orlando, FL: Harcourt, Brace. Henkes, K. (1991).
  Chrysthanthemum. New York: Scholastic.
Rogers, J. (1993). *Best friend's sleepover*. New York: Scholastic.
Say, A. (1989). *The lost lake*. Boston: Houghton Mifflin.

Inferencing:

Bunting, E. (1988). *How many days to America?: A Thanksgiving story*. New York: Clarion
  Books.
Danneberg, J. (2000). *First day jitters*. Watertown, MA: Charlesbridge.
Nelson, V. M. (2003). *Almost to freedom*. New York: Scholastic.
Woodson, J. (2004). *Coming on home soon*. New York: Scholastic.

Character Traits:

Jordan, D. (2000). *Salt in his shoes*. New York: Scholastic.
Polacco, P. (1998). *Thank you, Mr. Falker*. New York: Scholastic.
Polacco, P. (2001). *Mr. Lincoln's way*. New York: Scholastic.
San Souci, R. D. (1989). *The talking eggs*. New York: Penguin Putnam.

Visualization:

Brown, R. (1996). *TOAD*. New York: Scholastic.
Hest, A. (1997). *When Jessie came across the sea*. Cambridge, MA: Candlewick Press.
McPhail, D. (1997). *Edward and the pirates*. Singapore: Little, Brown.
Mitchell, M. K. (1993. *Uncle Jed's barbershop*. New York: Scholastic.
Murphy, J. (1989). *The call of the wolves*. New York: Scholastic.

Mood:

Yolen, J. (1987). *Owl moon*. New York: Scholastic.
Compare–Contrast:
San Soud, R. D. (1989). *The talking eggs*. New York: Penguin Putnam.

and . . .

Steptoe, J. (1987). *Mufaro's beautiful daughters*. New York: Scholastic.
Zelinsky, P. O. (1986). *Rumplestiltskin*. Boston: Houghton Mifflin.

and . . .

Hamilton, V. (2000). *The girl who spun gold*. New York: Blue Sky Press.

Organization:

Viorst, J. (1972). *Alexander and the terrible, horrible, no good, very bad day*. New York:
  Aladdin.

(continued)

FIGURE 7.8. Books in Mrs. Brennan's basket.

Transition Words:

Shannon, D. (1998). *A bad case of stripes.* New York: Scholastic.

Cause and Effect:

Dykes, T. T. (1951). *Faithful elephants: A true story of animals, people, and war.* Boston: Houghton Mifflin.

Wonders:

Van Allsburg, C. (1991). *The wretched stone.* Boston: Houghton Mifflin.

Word Choice:

Bedard, M. (1998). *Sitting ducks.* New York: Putnam & Grosset.

FIGURE 7.8. *(continued)*

REFERENCES

Almasi, J. F. (2002). Peer discussion. In B. Guzzetti (Ed.), *Literacy in America: An ency-clopedia* (Vol. 2, pp. 420-424). New York: ABC.

Almasi, J. F. (2003). *Teaching strategic processes in reading.* New York: Guilford Press.

Almasi, J. F. (in press). Using questioning strategies to promote students' active com-prehension of content area material. In D. Lapp & J. Flood (Eds.), *Content area reading instruction* (5th ed.).

Almasi, J. F., Palmer, B. M., Garas, K., Cho, H., Ma, W., Shanahan, L., et al. (2004, April). *A longitudinal investigation of peer discussion of text on reading development in grades K–3.* Final Report submitted to the Institute of Education Sciences, Washington, DC.

Anti-Defamation League. (2005, Winter). *Words that heal: Using children's literature to address bullying.* Retrieved November 8, 2005, from www.adl.org/education/cur-riculum_connections/winter_2005

Baumann, J. F., & Kame'enui, E. J. (Eds.). (2004). *Vocabulary instruction: Research to practice.* New York: Guilford Press.

Beach, R., & Hynds, S. (1991). Research on response to literature. In R. Barr, M. L. Kamil, P. B. Mosenthal, & P. D. Pearson (Eds.), *Handbook of reading research* (Vol. 2, pp. 453–489). New York: Longman.

Bear, D. R., Invernizzi, M., Templeton, S., & Johnston, F. (2000). *Words their way* (2nd ed.). Upper Saddle River, NJ: Prentice Hall.

Beaver, J. (2001). *Developmental reading assessment.* Lebanon, IN: Pearson.

Beck, I. L., McKeown, M. G., & Kucan, L. (2002). *Bringing words to life: Robust vocabu-lary instruction.* New York: Guilford Press.

Blachowicz, C. L. Z., & Fisher, P. (2004). Keep the "fun" in fundamental: Encouraging word awareness and incidental word learning in the classroom through word play. In J. F. Baumann & E. J. Kame'enui (Eds.), *Vocabulary instruction: Research to prac-tice* (pp. 218–237). New York: Guilford Press.

Bosch, C. W. (1988). *Bully on the bus*. Seattle, WA: Parenting Press.

Branley, F. M. (1985). *Flash, crash, rumble, and roll*. New York: HarperTrophy.

Briggs, R. (1978). *The snowman*. New York: Random House.

Calfee, R., & Hiebert, E. (1991). Classroom assessment of reading. In R. Barr, M. L. Kamil, P. Mosenthal, & P. D. Pearson (Eds.), *Handbook of reading research* (Vol. 2, pp. 281–309). New York: Longman.

Calkins, L. M. (1986). *The art of teaching writing*. Portsmouth, NH: Heinemann.

Carlisle, J. F., & Rice, M. S. (2004). Assessment of reading comprehension. In C. A. Stone, E. R. Silliman, B. J. Ehren, & K. Apel (Eds.), *Handbook of language and literacy: Development and disorders* (pp. 521–540). New York: Guilford Press.

Catling, P. S. (1952). *The chocolate touch*. New York: Dell Yearling.

Cazden, C. B. (1986). Classroom discourse. In M. C. Wittrock (Ed.), *Handbook of research on teaching* (3rd ed., pp. 432–463). New York: Macmillan.

Cazden, C. B. (1988). *Classroom discourse: The language of teaching and learning*. Portsmouth, NH: Heinemann.

Chall, J. S. (1996). *Stages of reading development* (2nd ed.). Fort Worth, TX: Harcourt-Brace.

Christopher, M. (1971). *Tough to tackle*. New York: Little, Brown.

Cleary, B. (1983). *Dear Mr. Henshaw*. New York: HarperTrophy.

Climo, S. (1989). *The Egyptian Cinderella*. New York: HarperCollins.

Climo, S. (1993). *The Korean Cinderella*. New York: HarperTrophy.

Climo, S. (1996). *The Irish Cinderlad*. New York: HarperCollins.

Climo, S. (1999). *The Persian Cinderella*. New York: HarperCollins.

Cole, A. D. (2002). *Better answers: Written performance that looks good and sounds smart*. Portland, ME: Stenhouse.

Cole, A. D. (2003). *Knee to knee, eye to eye: Circling in on comprehension*. Portsmouth, NH: Heinemann.

Cole, J. E. (2002). What motivates students to read? Four literacy personalities. *The Reading Teacher, 56*(4), 326–336.

Cole, M., & Cole, S. R. (2001). *The development of children* (4th ed.). New York: Worth.

Corcoran, B. (1969). *Sasha my friend*. New York: Atheneum.

Craft, K. Y. (2000). *Cinderella*. New York: Seastar Books.

Creech, S. (2001). *Love that dog*. New York: HarperCollins.

Dahl, R. (1988). *Fantastic Mr. Fox*. New York: Puffin Books.

Dakos, K. (1990). *If you're not here, please raise your hand: Poems about school*. New York: Aladdin.

Daneman, M. (1991). Individual differences in reading skills. In R. Barr, M. L. Kamil, P. B. Mosenthal, & P. D. Pearson (Eds.), *Handbook of Reading Research* (Vol. 2, pp. 512–538). White Plains, NY: Longman.

dePaola, T. (1978). *Pancakes for breakfast*. New York: Voyager Books.

dePaola, T. (1979). *Oliver Button is a sissy*. New York: Harcourt, Brace.

DiCamillo, K. (2000). *Because of Winn Dixie*. Cambridge, MA: Candlewick Press.

Dillon, J. T. (1985). Using questions to foil discussion. *Teaching and Teacher Education, 1*, 109–121.

Dole, J. A., Brown, K. J., & Trathen, W. (1996). The effects of strategy instruction on the comprehension performance of at-risk students. *Reading Research Quarterly, 31*(1), 62–88.

Duffy, G. G., Roehler, L. R., Sivan, E., Rackliffe, G., Book, C., Meloth, M. S., et al. (1987). Effects of explaining the reasoning associated with using reading strategies. *Reading Research Quarterly, 22*(3), 347–368.

Durkin, D. (1978/79). What classroom observations reveal about reading comprehension instruction. *Reading Research Quarterly, 15,* 481-533.

Edwards, E. C., Font, G., Baumann, J. F., & Boland, E. (2004).Unlocking word meanings: Strategies and guidelines for teaching morphemic and contextual analysis. In J. F. Baumann & E. J. Kame'enui (Eds.), *Vocabulary instruction: Research to practice* (pp. 159–176). New York: Guilford Press.

Ehri, L. C. (1991). Development of the ability to read words. In R. Barr, M. L. Kamil, P. B. Mosenthal, & P. D. Pearson (Eds.), *Handbook of reading research* (Vol. 2, pp. 383–417). New York: Longman.

Eldridge, J. L., Reutzel, D. R., & Hollingsworth, P. M. (1996). Comparing the effectiveness of two oral reading practices: Round-robin reading and the shared book experience. *Journal of Literacy Research, 28*(2), 201–225.

Erikson, E. (1963). *Childhood and society* (2nd ed.). New York: Norton.

Estes, E. (1974). *The hundred dresses.* New York: Harcourt, Brace.

Fielding, L. G., & Pearson, P. D. (1994). Reading comprehension: What works. *Educational Leadership, 51,* 62–68.

Flavell, J. H. (1985). *Cognitive development* (2nd ed.). Englewood Cliffs, NJ: Prentice Hall.

Fleischman, P. (1988). *Joyful noise: Poems for two voices.* New York: HarperTrophy.

Fleischman, S. (1986). *The whipping boy.* New York: Greenwillow Books.

Flood, J., Lapp, D., Flood, S., & Nagel, G. (1992). Am I allowed to group? Using flexible patterns for effective instruction. *The Reading Teacher, 45*(8), 608–615.

Fountas, I. C., & Pinnell, G. S. (1996). *Guided reading: Good first teaching for all children.* Portsmouth, NH: Heinemann.

Fountas, I. C., & Pinnell, G. S. (2001). *Guiding readers and writers: Grades 3–6, teaching comprehension, genre, and content literacy.* Portsmouth, NH: Heinemann.

Fox, B. J. (2000). *Word identification strategies: Phonics from a new perspective* (2nd ed.). Upper Saddle River, NJ: Merrill.

Galdone, P. (1970). *The three little pigs.* New York: Houghton Mifflin.

Gambrell, L. B., & Almasi, J. F. (1996). *Lively discussions! Fostering engaged readers.* Newark, DE: International Reading Association.

Gambrell, L. B., Palmer, B. M., Codling, R. M., & Mazzoni, S. A. (1996). Assessing motivation to read. *The Reading Teacher, 49*(7), 518–533.

Gardner, J. R. (1980). *Stone fox.* New York: HarperCollins.

Garner, R. (1987). *Metacognition and reading comprehension.* Norwood, NJ: Ablex.

Gaskins, I. W. (2003). Reading for comprehension. In A. P. Sweet & C. E. Snow (Eds.), *Rethinking reading comprehension* (pp. 141–165). New York: Guilford Press.

Gelman, R., & Baillargeon, R. (1983). A review of some Piagetian concepts. In P. Mussen (Ed.), E. Markman & J. Flavell (Vol. Eds.), *Carmichael's manual of child psychology: Vol. 3. Cognitive development.* New York: Wiley.

Gibbons, G. (1991). *From seed to plant.* New York: Holiday House.

Gibbons, G. (1992). *Recycle! A handbook for kids.* New York: Little, Brown.

Gibbons, G. (1993). *Spiders.* New York: Holiday House.

Gibbons, G. (1995). *The reasons for seasons.* New York: Holiday House.

Gibbons, G. (1996). *Deserts*. New York: Holiday House.

Gillett, J. W., & Temple, C. (1994). *Understanding reading problems: Assessment and instruction*. New York: HarperCollins.

Goodman, Y. M., & Marek, A. M. (1996). Retrospective miscue analysis. In Y. M. Goodman & A. M. Marek (Eds.), *Retrospective miscue analysis revaluing readers and reading* (pp. 39–47). Katonah, NY: Richard C. Owen.

Graves, M. F. (2004). Teaching prefixes: As good as it gets? In J. F. Baumann & E. J. Kame'enui (Eds.), *Vocabulary instruction: Research to practice* (pp. 81–99). New York: Guilford Press.

Griffith, L. W., & Rasinski, T. (2004). A focus on fluency: How one teacher incorporated fluency with her reading curriculum. *The Reading Teacher, 58*(2), 126–137.

Harris, T. L., & Hodges, R. E. (1995). *The literacy dictionary: The vocabulary of reading and writing*. Newark, DE: International Reading Association.

Harvey, S., & Goudvis, A. (2000). *Strategies that work*. Portland, ME: Stenhouse.

Heacox, D. (2002). *Differentiating instruction in the regular classroom*. Minneapolis, MN: Free Spirit.

Hickox, R. (1998). *The golden sandal: A Middle Eastern Cinderella story*. New York: Holiday House.

Hudson, R. F., Lane, H. B., & Pullen, P. C. (2005). Reading fluency assessment and instruction: What, why, and how? *The Reading Teacher, 58*(8), 702–714.

Hudson, W. (1993). *Pass it on: African-American poetry for children*. New York: Scholastic.

Hutchins, P. (1968). *Rosie's walk*. New York: Simon & Schuster.

Jacobs, H. H. (1997). *Mapping the big picture*. Alexandria, VA: Association for Supervision and Curriculum Development.

Jenkins, S. (2004). *Actual size*. Boston: Houghton Mifflin.

Johns, J. (2005). *Basic reading inventory: Preprimer through grade twelve and early literacy assessments* (9th ed.). Dubuque, IA: Kendall Hunt.

Johnston, P. H. (1997). *Knowing literacy: Constructive literacy assessment*. Portland, ME: Stenhouse.

Kalman, B. (1998). *What is a biome?* New York: Crabtree.

Kalman, B. (2000). *What is a plant?* New York: Crabtree.

Kalman, B., & Crossingham, J. (2001). *What are camouflage and mimicry?* New York: Crabtree.

Kalman, B., & Everts, T. (1994). *Frogs and toads*. New York: Crabtree.

Kalman, B., & Langille, J. (1998). *What are food chains and webs?* New York: Crabtree.

Kalman, B., & Langille, J. (1998). *What is a life cycle?* New York: Crabtree.

Kindermann, T. (2003). Children's relationships and development of person–context relations. In J. Valsiner & K. Connolly (Eds.), *Handbook of developmental psychology* (pp. 407–430). London: Sage.

Klenk, L., & Almasi, J. F. (1997). School-based practicum in reading disabilities. *The Language and Literacy Spectrum, 7*, 73–79.

Konigsburg, E. L. (1967). *Jennifer, Hecate, MacBeth, William McKinley and Me Elizabeth*. New York: Bantam Doubleday Dell Books.

Krashen, S. D. (2004). *The power of reading: Insights from the research* (2nd ed.). Portsmouth, NH: Heinemann/Libraries Unlimited.

Kucan, L., & Beck, I. L. (1997). Thinking aloud and reading comprehension research: Inquiry, instruction, and social interaction. *Review of Educational Research, 67*(3), 271–299.

Kuhn, M. R., & Stahl, S. (2003). Fluency: A review of developmental and remedial strategies. *The Journal of Educational Psychology. 95*, 1–19.

LaBerge, D., & Samuels, S. J. (1974). Toward a theory of automatic information processing in reading. *Cognitive Psychology, 6*, 293–323.

Langer, J. A. (1992). Rethinking literature instruction. In J. A. Langer (Ed.), *Literature instruction: A focus on student response* (pp. 35–53). Urbana, IL: National Council of Teachers of English.

Leslie, L., & Caldwell, J. (2006). *Qualitative reading inventory–4* (4th ed.). Boston, MA: Allyn & Bacon.

Lipson, M. Y. (1996). Conversations with children and other classroom-based assessment strategies. In L. R. Putnam (Ed.), *How to become a better reading teacher: Strategies for assessment and intervention* (pp. 167–179). Englewood Cliffs, NJ: Merrill.

Louie, A. (1987). *Yeh-Shen: A Cinderella story from China.* New York: Puffin Books.

Ludwig, T. (2003). *My secret bully.* Berkeley, CA: Tricycle Press.

Marshall, J. (2000). Research on response to literature. In M. L. Kamil, P. B. Mosenthal, P. D. Pearson, & R. Barr (Eds.), *Handbook of reading research* (Vol. 3, pp. 381–402). Mahwah, NJ: Erlbaum.

Martin, A. (2000). *The doll people.* New York: Hyperion.

Martin, R. (1992). *The rough face girl.* New York: Penguin Putnam Books.

Marzano, R. J. (2004). The developing vision of vocabulary instruction. In J. F. Baumann & E. J. Kame'enui (Eds.), *Vocabulary instruction: Research to practice* (pp. 100–117). New York: Guilford Press.

Matanzo, J. (1996). Discussion: Assessing what was said and what was done. In L. B. Gambrell & J. F. Almasi (Eds.), *Lively discussions: Fostering engaged reading* (pp. 250–264). Newark, DE: International Reading Association.

McCain, B. R. (2001). *Nobody knew what to do.* Morton Grove, IL: Whitman.

McCully, E. A. (1985). *First snow.* New York: HarperTrophy.

McDevitt, T. M., & Ormrod, J. E. (2002). *Child development and education.* Upper Saddle River, NJ: Pearson Education.

McKenna, M. C., & Kear, D. J. (1990). Measuring attitude toward reading: A new tool for teachers. *The Reading Teacher, 43*(8), 626–639.

McKenna, M. C., Kear, D. J., & Ellsworth, R. A. (1995). Children's attitudes toward reading: A national survey. *Reading Research Quarterly, 30*(4), 934–956.

McKeown, M. G., & Beck. I. L. (2004). Direct and rich vocabulary instruction. In J. F. Baumann & E. J. Kame'enui (Eds.), *Vocabulary instruction: Research to practice* (pp. 13–27). New York: Guilford Press.

McNamee, G. (2000). *Nothing wrong with a three-legged dog.* New York: Yearling.

Mehan, H. (1979). *Learning lessons.* Cambridge, MA: Harvard University Press.

Meyer, B. J. F. (1975). Identification of the structure of prose and its implications for the study of reading and memory. *Journal of Reading Behavior, 7*, 7–48.

Mohr, N. (1979). *Felita.* New York: Puffin Books.

Morrow, L. M. (1996). Story retelling: A discussion strategy to develop and assess comprehension. In L. B. Gambrell and J. F. Almasi (Eds.), *Lively discussions: Fostering engaged reading* (pp. 265–285). Newark, DE: International Reading Association.

Morrow, L. M. (2002). *The literacy center: Contexts for reading and writing* (2nd ed.). Portland, ME: Stenhouse.

Moskal, B. M. (2000a). *Scoring rubrics. Part I: What and when.* ERIC/AE Digest. (ERIC Document ED446110).

Moskal, B. M. (2000b). *Scoring rubrics. Part II: How?* ERIC/AE Digest. (ERIC Document ED446111).

Moss, M. P. (2004). *Say something.* Gardiner, ME: Tilbury House.

Myers, C. (2000). *Wings.* New York: Scholastic.

Myller, R. (1962). *How big is a foot?* New York: Dell.

National Center for Education Statistics. (2004a). *National assessment of educational progress: The nation's report card reading highlights 2003.* Washington, DC: U.S. Department of Education Institute of Education Sciences. Retrieved October 27, 2004, from nces.ed.gov/nationsreportcard/reading/results2003

National Center for Education Statistics. (2004b). *Progress in International Reading Literacy Study 2001.* Washington, DC: U.S. Department of Education Institute of Education Sciences. Retrieved October 27, 2004, from nces.ed.gov/pubs2004/pirlspub/index.asp

National Reading Panel (2000). *Report of the National Reading Panel: Teaching children to read: An evidence-based assessment of the scientific research literature on reading and its implications for reading instruction.* Rockville, MD: National Institute of Child Health and Human Development, National Institute for Literacy, and the U.S. Department of Health and Human Services.

Neuman, S. B. (1999). Books make a difference: A study of access to literacy. *Reading Research Quarterly, 34*(3), 286–311.

O'Connor, J. (1988). *Sir Small and the dragonfly.* New York: Random House.

Ogle, D. M. (1986). K-W-L: A teaching model that develops active reading of expository text. *The Reading Teacher, 39*(6), 564–570.

Opitz, M. F., & Rasinski, T. V. (1998). *Good-bye round robin: 25 effective oral reading strategies.* Portsmouth, NH: Heinemann.

Osborne, M. P. (1998). *Vacation under the Volcano.* New York: Random House.

Pearson, P. D., & Dole, J. A. (1987). Explicit comprehension instruction: A review of research and a new conceptualization of instruction. *The Elementary School Journal, 88*(2), 151–165.

Pearson, P. D., & Fielding, L. (1991). Comprehension instruction. In R. Barr, M. L. Kamil, P. Mosenthal, & P. D. Pearson (Eds.), *Handbook of reading research* (Vol. 2, pp. 815–860). New York: Longman.

Pearson, P. D., & Gallagher, M. C. (1983). The instruction of reading comprehension. *Contemporary Educational Psychology, 8,* 317–344.

Pearson, P. D., & Hamm, D. N. (2005). The assessment of reading comprehension: A review of practices—past, present, and future. In S. G. Paris & S. A. Stahl (Eds.), *Children's reading comprehension and assessment* (pp. 13–69). Mahwah, NJ: Erlbaum.

Perie, M., Grigg, W., & Donahue, P. (2005). *The nation's report card: Reading 2005* (NCES 2006-451). Washington, DC: U.S. Department of Education, National Center for Education Statistics, U.S. Government Printing Office.

Perrault, C. (1999). *Cinderella*. New York: North-South Books.

Pollacco, P. (1988). *The keeping quilt*. New York: Simon & Schuster.

Pollock, P. (1996). *The turkey girl: A Zuni Cinderella story*. New York: Little, Brown.

Prawat, R. S. (1989). Promoting access to knowledge, strategy, and disposition in students: A research synthesis. *Review of Educational Research, 59*(1), 1–41.

Pressley, M. (2000). What should comprehension instruction be the instruction of? In M. L. Kamil, P. B. Mosenthal, P. D. Pearson, & R. Barr (Eds.), *Handbook of reading research* (Vol. 3, pp. 545–561). Mahwah, NJ: Erlbaum.

Pressley, M., & Afflerbach, P. P. (1995). *Verbal protocols of reading: The nature of constructively responsive reading*. Hillsdale, NJ: Erlbaum.

Rasinski, T. V., & Padak, N. (1996). *Holistic reading strategies: Teaching children who find reading difficult*. Englewood Cliffs, NJ: Merrill/Prentice Hall.

Rasinski, T. V., Padak, N., Linek, W., & Sturtevant, E. (1994). Effects of fluency development on urban second-grade readers. *Journal of Educational Research, 87*, 158–165.

Sachar, L. (1998). *Holes*. New York: Dell Yearling.

San Souci, R. D. (1998). *Cendrillon: A Caribbean Cinderella*. New York: Simon & Schuster.

Schroeder, A. (1997). *Smoky Mountain Rose: An Appalachian Cinderella*. New York: Puffin Books.

Schwanenflugel, P. J., Hamilton, A. M., Kuhn, M. R., Wisenbaker, J. M., & Stahl, S. A. (2004). Becoming a fluent reader: Reading skill and prosodic features in the oral reading of young readers. *Journal of Educational Psychology, 96*(1), 119–129.

Scott, J. A., & Nagy, W. E. (1989, December). *Fourth graders' knowledge of definitions and how they work*. Paper presented at the annual meeting of the National Reading Conference, Austin, TX.

Selman, R. L. (1981). The child as a friendship philosopher. In S. R. Asher & J. M. Gottman (Eds.), *The development of children's friendships*. Cambridge, UK: Cambridge University Press.

Sigmon, C., & Ford, S. (2002). *Writing mini-lessons for third grade*. Greensboro, NC: Carson-Dellosa.

Silver, H., Strong, R., & Perini, M. (2001). *Tools for promoting active, in-depth learning*. Ho Ho Kus, NJ: Thoughtful Education Press.

Silverstein, S. (1974). *Where the sidewalk ends*. New York: HarperCollins.

Smith, D. B. (1973). *A taste of blackberries*. New York: HarperCollins.

Snicket, L. (1999). *A series of unfortunate events*. New York: Scholastic.

Snow, C. E., Burns, M. S., & Griffin, P. (1998). *Preventing reading difficulties in young children*. Washington, DC: National Academy Press.

Snow, C. E., & Sweet, A. P. (2003). Reading for comprehension. In A. P. Sweet & C. E. Snow (Eds.), *Rethinking reading comprehension* (pp. 1–11). New York: Guilford Press.

Speare, E. G. (1983). *The sign of the beaver*. New York: Dell Yearling.

Taba, H. (1967). *Teacher's handbook for elementary social studies*. Reading, MA: Addison-Wesley.

Taback, S. (1997). *There was an old lady who swallowed a fly*. New York: Viking.

Taberski, S. (2000). *On solid ground: Strategies for teaching reading K–3*. Portsmouth, NH: Heinemann.

Taylor, B., Frye, B. J., & Maruyama, G. (1990). Time spent reading and reading growth. *American Educational Research Journal, 27*(2), 351–362.

Taylor, M. D. (1976). *Roll of thunder, hear my cry.* New York: Puffin Books.

Taylor, M. D. (1990). *Mississippi bridge.* New York: Bantam Books.

Third-grade writing rubric. (n.d.). Retrieved October 23, 2005, from rubistar.4teachers. org/index.php

Tierney, R. J., Carter, M. A., & Desai, L. E. (1991). *Portfolio assessment in the reading-writing classroom.* Norwood, MA: Christopher-Gordon.

Tomlinson, C. A. (1999). *The differentiated classroom.* Alexandria, VA: Association for Supervision and Curriculum Development.

Tompkins, G. E. (2000). *Teaching writing: Balancing process and product* (3rd ed.). Upper Saddle River, NJ: Merrill.

Tompkins, G. E., & McGee, L. M. (1992). *Teaching reading with literature: Case studies to action plans.* Upper Saddle River, NJ: Prentice Hall.

Tompkins, G. E., & McGee, L. M. (1993). *Teaching reading with literature: Case studies to action plans.* New York: Merrill.

Turner, J., & Paris, S. G. (1995). How literacy tasks influence children's motivation for literacy. *The Reading Teacher, 48*(8), 662–673.

Turner, J. C. (1995). The influence of classroom contexts on young children's motivation for literacy. *Reading Research Quarterly, 30*(3), 410–441.

Viorst, J. (1972). *Alexander and the terrible, horrible, no good, very bad day.* New York: Aladdin.

Vygotsky, L. S. (1978). *Mind in society.* Cambridge, MA: Harvard University Press.

Wade, S. E. (1990). Using think alouds to assess comprehension. *The Reading Teacher, 43*(7), 442–451.

Wadsworth, B. J. (1984). *Piaget's theory of cognitive and affective development* (3rd ed.). New York: Longman.

Walker, B. J. (2000). *Diagnostic teaching of reading: Techniques for instruction and assessment* (4th ed.). Upper Saddle River, NJ: Merrill.

Weiner, B. (1986). *An attributional theory of motivation and emotion.* New York: Springer-Verlag.

Williams, L. (1986). *The little old lady who was not afraid of anything.* New York: HarperCollins.

Wolf, S. A. (2004). *Interpreting literature with children.* Mahwah, NJ: Erlbaum.

Woolfolk, A. E. (1998). *Educational psychology* (7th ed.). Boston, MA: Allyn & Bacon.

Worthy, J., & Broaddus, K. (2002). Fluency beyond the primary grades: From group performance to silent, independent reading. *The Reading Teacher, 55*(4), 334–342.

Worthy, J., & Prater, K. (2002). "I thought about it all night": Readers theatre for reading fluency and motivation. *The Reading Teacher, 56*(3), 294–297.

Zoehfeld, K. W. (1995). *How mountains are made.* New York: HarperCollins.

INDEX